Harry Strugnell
Kelseyville, Calif.
279-4364

GREATEST MOMENTS IN
GOLF

GREATEST MOMENTS IN
GOLF

PAUL GREGORY

Exeter Books

NEW YORK

A Bison Book

Page 1: Severiano Ballesteros puts everything into a drive during the 1979 British Open, his first major success.
Pages 2-3: Packed crowds revel in the action during the 1985 Ryder Cup.
Pages 4-5: Bobby Jones teeing off at the 17th on his way to winning the 1927 British Open at St Andrews with a record score of 285.

CONTENTS

INTRODUCTION

Picking the greatest moments in any sport is never easy. Picking golf's greatest moments is, perhaps, harder than any other sport – there have been so many great moments provided by a host of *greats* over the years.

The Great Triumvirate of Braid, Taylor and Vardon at the turn of the century were the first of the great golfers. But the British dominance in the United States was shattered by one Francis D. Ouimet in 1913, when, as a 20-year-old amateur he beat the pick of the Britons, Ted Ray and Harry Vardon, in a play-off to win the US Open title. Since then, the United States has remained top of the golfing world – with the exception of the odd South African, European or Australian who has dared threaten this domination.

Walter Hagen followed Ouimet as US Open champion and went on to win 10 more majors up to 1929. But the 1920s belonged to one man – Robert Tyre 'Bobby' Jones.

A brilliant academic, Jones held degrees in literature, engineering and law and on the golf course he was unrivalled. He won the US Open four times, the US Amateur title five times, the British Open three times, and the British Amateur title once. He crowned a great career by winning all four titles in one year, 1930. Even today, long after his death, Bobby Jones is still talked about as the greatest golfer ever seen. If records alone are a criterion for such a statement, he certainly *was* the greatest.

Such notable post-war players as Ben Hogan and Sam Snead have challenged for Jones' title. Their dominance of the immediate post-war years led to them winning 15 majors between 1946-54. But, when looking for one of golf's greatest moments, Ben Hogan's 1950 US Open win less than twelve months after being left for dead following a car accident, must surely rank high among candidates.

The coming of golf's second great 'Triumvirate' – Arnold Palmer, Jack Nicklaus and Gary Player – brought about many magic moments. Each could easily fill a book in his own right. Now, 25 years after their emergence, Nicklaus is still providing great moments – his 1986 US Masters win is full testament.

In addition to those three immortals, the golf world has been privileged to be blessed with such stars as Tom Watson, Tom Weiskopf, Lee Trevino, Johnny Miller, Severiano Ballesteros, Bernhard Langer, Greg Norman, and many more. They have all added their own brand and style of play to the great sport.

Every one of the above mentioned, and many more as well, have provided the galleries with great moments over the years. So where does one begin to pick golf's greatest moments? Furthermore, what is a great moment?

Gene Sarazen's hole-in-one at Troon's Postage Stamp hole in the 1973 British Open was a great moment shared by millions of television viewers. Bobby Jones' remarkable Grand Slam in 1930 was another of golf's great moments. Sarazen's moment of glory lasted seconds . . . Jones' lasted a season. So, we still have the question: What is a great moment?

The selection on the following pages is not the definitive list of greatest golfing moments – such a list is impossible. Obtaining universal agreement on such a list is also impossible. But one thing is certain, each of the entries has provided golf with that special piece of nostalgia and will, I hope make enjoyable reading.

Paul Gregory

Left: One of golf's great characters, Lee Trevino.
Below: Another true great, 'Slammin' Sam Snead.

Below: Severiano Ballesteros (left) receiving the winner's green jacket from the 1982 Masters champion Craig Stadler.

BOBBY JONES' GRAND SLAM YEAR

Bobby Jones competed in his first US Amateur Championship at Merion in 1916 when only 14 years of age and when he first won the championship eight years later it was over the same Philadelphia course. It was, therefore, more than appropriate that in 1930 Merion should be the scene of the climax to the greatest-ever golfing feat when Jones completed his Grand Slam of British Amateur, British Open, US Open and US Amateur championship wins in one year.

Robert Tyre Jones junior was born in Atlanta, Georgia, in 1902. A brilliant student, he obtained degrees in engineering, law and literature and his golf was on a par with his scholastic achievements. Jones remained an amateur throughout his entire career, but dominated both the professional and amateur game in the 1920s. His swing was one of perfection and he duly earned the title of the world's greatest golfer. His performance in winning the Open Championships of the United States and Great Britain, as well as the amateur championships of both countries, within a four-month period has remained unparalleled in the golfing world.

Jones became US Open champion at Inwood in 1923 when he beat Bobby Cruickshank in a play-off and he won the US Amateur title the next two years, on each occasion at a Pennsylvania course – Merion and Oakmont. He came close to achieving the Grand Slam in 1926 when he won the US Open at Scioto and his first British Open at Royal Lytham but defeat in the final of the US Amateur by George Von Elm and a sixth-round elimination in the British Amateur championship prevented a remarkable achievement. Further US and British Open titles followed, as did two more US Amateur titles before he set about his assault on all four titles, once more, in 1930.

Jones travelled to Britain with the US Walker Cup team and helped them to a comfortable 10-2 win at St George's, Sandwich – in which he beat Roger Wethered 9 & 8 in the singles, and, with his partner Dr Willing, beat Rex Hartley and Tony Torrance 8 & 7 in the foursomes. Jones then travelled north of the border to the home of golf, St Andrews, for the British Amateur championship. Jones loved St Andrews, and St Andrews loved Jones and the Scottish fans dearly wanted him to win the one trophy that had so far eluded him.

On the Saturday before the championship, Scotland played England in an amateur international over the St Andrews links. Jones followed the participat-

Above: Jones (teeing off), with, from left, Tommy Armour,
Walter Hagen and Gene Sarazen in 1935.
Left: Jones captained the US Walker Cup team to victory at
Sandwich before going to St Andrews.

ing players round the course, playing a friendly fourball with St Andrews' committee members, and their
match attracted a bigger gallery than any players in
the international!

The championship got under way on Monday 26
May and the course was looking as magnificent as
ever. In fact, it looked as good that May as in September when it usually reaches its peak. The greens were
fast, but true, and the tees were farther back than
usual to make it most testing.

Jones had a bye in the first round and went out at
3.00 pm on the first day for his second-round match
against S. Roper, whose biggest claim to fame was
being drawn against Jones. A gray morning had
turned into afternoon sunshine, and conditions were
described as being 'ideal American golfing weather.'
It certainly helped the three of the eight American
challengers who were playing that afternoon – they
all won.

Roper had a chance to get his moment of glory but
could not capitalize on it. He played brilliantly on the
day and, under normal circumstances, would have
won his match but Jones was at his mercurial best to
win 3 & 2. When play finished at the 16th, Jones was
four under fours and that included a five at the short
eighth. Jones opened 3-4-3-2 to Roper's 4-4-4-4 to
build up a lead of three after just four holes and there
seemed to be no way the Nottinghamshire player was
going to overcome that handicap, and he did not.

Jones was not in action on the second day, which
was fortunate because the wind changed from east to
west, making certain holes particularly hazardous so
that even good players were made to look like high
handicap club golfers. When Jones teed off at 8.12 am
for his third round match on the third day, overcoats
and mittens were evident among the crowd. The
strong west wind was still blowing and made conditions very cold. Jones was visibly upset by the miserable weather and his early start when he arrived at the
first tee.

The conditions got to the American and he played poorly by his standards. Fortunately, so did his
opponent C. Shankland of St George's Hill who, had

he played moderately well, could possibly have won. Jones started with three straight fours which, surprisingly, won him each hole, but then Shankland retaliated with wins at the fourth and fifth. Jones was one up at the turn (despite going out in 40!) but he won the first two inward holes and after that there was never any doubt about the result and Jones finally won 3 & 2.

A difficult fourth round match against England's Cyril Tolley followed that same afternoon. Conditions were still dreadful, but the two players provided great golf for the large gallery. It was a holiday in nearby Dundee and the attendance was swelled by the day-trippers. The crowd was so vast that play was difficult for Jones and Tolley: it was virtually impossible for other players out on the course.

Jones and Tolley had figured in the Walker Cup at Sandwich, and both showed why they were international golfers. Jones won the first hole with a four to a five after Tolley topped his tee shot. But Tolley level-

led it at the second and that was to be the pattern for the 18 holes, with neither letting the other get away.

Tolley took the lead at the fourth and held it until the seventh. After that Jones regained the advantage and never allowed his English opponent to take the lead again. Tolley drew level for the fifth time at the 16th and after two pars each it went to a sudden death play-off. And it was sad that such a great match was ended with Jones winning after laying a now-outlawed stymie to clinch the hole and a place in the fifth round.

In the fifth round Jones had a 7 & 6 win over G. O. Watt in what the boxing world would describe as a 'no contest.' Jones stamped his superiority between the 6th and 11th holes when he had four threes. It was a different matter that afternoon, however, as he had to play the first of his American opponents, Harrison Johnston from Minnesota. Johnston, the reigning US Amateur champion, was not going to let Jones have

such an easy time as Watt did in the morning and the result of their match was in doubt up to the final hole.

A huge gallery attended the first all-American clash of the tournament, and it was a more sedate St Andrews crowd rather than the unruly Dundee crowd who had gone home. Both men played well but Jones

Below: Roger Wethered, seen watching George Von Elm teeing off during the 1930 Walker Cup, was the last man to stand in Jones' way when Jones won the Amateur title at St Andrews, but was no match for the great American.

just had that edge. He led by one at the half-way stage, but had increased the lead to four holes at the end of the 13th. Johnston won 14 and 15 and then dropped a 12-foot putt at the 16th for a half when it looked as though all was lost. Johnston pulled one more back at the 17th, the famous Road Hole, with a perfect four. And so, with one to go, Jones was still hanging on to his slender lead.

Johnston put the pressure on Jones by sinking his putt for par and the Atlantan had a difficult putt for a half. Considering the pressure, it was a remarkable effort from Jones, who sank it for the half and the match. Jones immediately fled for the clubhouse before the army of fans could mob him.

Jones was now just three matches away from winning the elusive title and on the Friday two men stood in his way of reaching the final. They were Eric Fiddian of England and fellow American Walker Cup player George Voigt.

The morning match with Fiddian proved no obstacle as Jones played consistently to beat the courageous youngster 4 & 3. Voigt, however, proved to be a tougher opponent and when Voigt led by two with five to play, there seemed little chance of Jones making the final ... but you never write off Bobby Jones.

Both players had seemed frightened of each other to begin with but Voigt gained the advantage after Jones' short putting had let him down, and going to the 14th Voigt was two up, but he then drove out of bounds. Jones had a chance to level the match at 15 but again missed a short putt. Jones did level at the 16th when Voigt went into the notorious 'Principal's Nose' bunker.

Jones holed a pressure putt at the Road Hole to stay level and then, at the 18th he delivered a killer-blow when he holed an eight-footer. Voigt had to sink his putt from six feet to stay in the match, but he missed and Jones was in the final.

Jones' opponent in the 36-hole final was Roger Wethered, whom he had beaten 9 & 8 in the Walker Cup. But despite him being the best match-play golfer in England, Wethered was no match for the 'Master' as Jones swept him aside with another big win. Jones played the opening nine holes without a flaw in his game and, although both men went out in 35, Wethered had to work hard for his score. The second nine saw Jones win four holes in succession to build up a lead. Wethered started the second 18 with a win but Jones pulled that back at the next hole. Wethered never gave up and managed to win the 24th, but Jones struck back immediately. He then went on to win at 28 and 30 to clinch the match 7 & 6. During his round of 30 holes Jones had 22 fours.

And so, the dream of winning the British Amateur championship was reality as Jones made his way back to the clubhouse under a guard of four local constables who tried to control the massive crowd. The St Andrews crowd was delighted that Jones had, at last, won the title – and on their sacred course.

With that one out of the way Jones then turned his attention to the 'impossible' dream – of winning all four titles in one season. The British Open over the Royal Liverpool links at Hoylake was to be his next challenge.

Hoylake, and the nearby Wallasey links, staged the two qualifying rounds that reduced the 296 entrants to 100 or so. Jones had a 73 at Hoylake and 77 at Wallasey to qualify easily on 150, nine behind the top qualifier, Archie Compston.

The famous Wirral course had been staging the British Open since 1897, when local amateur Harold Horsfall Hilton won the title. Hoylake had played host to the Open four times since then and the last time had been in 1924 when Walter Hagen won his second title. Hagen, the defending champion, was not at Hoylake in 1930, but there was, nevertheless, a strong contingent of challengers from across the Atlantic. However, Jones was one of the favorites to

Top: Macdonald Smith nearly upset Jones' plans in the British Open, and
Above: ... so did fellow American George Voigt in the Amateur championship.
Above right: Britain's Henry Cotton was one of the biggest threats to Jones after the first round at Hoylake, but dropped away after an opening 70.
Right: Jones in action during the 1930 Walker Cup.

win the title for a third time to add to his 1926 and 1927 successes.

The 6750-yard course was made to seem even longer when the sultry weather of the first morning turned into a thunderstorm in the afternoon but Jones returned a magnificent 70 despite starting with two fives in the first three holes. His iron play and putting were superb and, but for some bad luck with his long putts, Jones could have developed an outright lead. Britain's Henry Cotton and American Macdonald Smith also returned opening scores of 70 to become the biggest threat to Jones.

It was ironic that before the start of play Jones confided to a friend that he never felt *less* confident about winning.

The second day was, again, sultry with a hint of thunder in the air and Jones started off badly once more, with 5-4-6 but played superbly in the second nine to come home with a 35 to add to his outward 37. It was sufficient to give him the outright lead on 142, one ahead of Fred Robson and three ahead of the new American challenger Horton Smith. Henry Cotton fell away with a 79 and Macdonald Smith had a 77 for an aggregate 147.

With two bad starts, and still leading, the crowd was asking: 'What will happen when he starts to play well?'

The next day he did, for a change, start well, but then tangled with trouble midway through the first nine holes. Then, within ten holes, he turned his score from three over fours to two under and was heading for a final score of 70 or 71 when disaster struck again and he finished with a couple of fives for 74. Once more Jones had not played his best golf, but

this time it cost him the lead, as top qualifier Archie Compston came in with a 68 for a 215 to Jones' 216. Compston had been five behind Jones at the start of the third round and was still two behind after nine but had a devastating second nine to pull back three shots. Only a six at the 16th cost him a championship record 66.

The final day was a complete disaster for Compston who shot an 82 for a final total of 297, which was to put him in joint sixth place. And that left the way clear for Jones, though once more he did not play at his best, to gain a clear-cut victory.

His approach shots let him down and it gave Leo Diegel and Macdonald Smith the opportunity to put pressure on him. But Jones responded every time they got within reach by producing that extra bit of magic.

Jones was in with 75 for 291 and the leader in the clubhouse. Only Diegel could catch him and, despite a brave effort, which needed only four 4s in the final five holes, he let his chance slip when he found the bunker at the 16th for a six. And that was the end of his gallant effort as Jones won the second leg of his Grand Slam, despite playing perhaps the poorest consecutive four rounds of his competitive career. In winning the British Amateur and Open titles Jones emulated the feat of the great English amateur John Ball 40 years earlier.

Above: Jones playing a mashie approach shot on a daisy and divot-ridden St Andrews!
Above right: Jones is presented with the 1930 British Open Championship trophy, the famous claret jug.

After a three-week lay-off Jones returned to the task of attempting to win the Grand Slam at the Interlachen course in Minnesota where the US Open was the third hurdle.

Jones came to the Minnesota course as defending champion, following his play-off win over Al Espinosa at Winged Foot twelve months earlier, but the European tour had taken a lot out of Jones and many thought that, despite him being the best player at the time, he was tired and would be struggling to win at Interlachen. On the contrary, Jones was back to his brilliant best after playing some disappointing golf in Europe.

By contrast to the dismal weather in Europe, the sun shone in Minnesota and Jones was troubled by sunburn during his final practice round which established a new course record of 70. The city of Minneapolis had played host to many championships on its eight courses, but this was the first time the Interlachen course had been privileged to be selected as the venue for the Open.

Any trouble Jones had with his woods in Europe was now well and truly patched up as that side of his game was as good as ever. He was only off the fairway with three tee shots in his first round of 71, just one behind the two Scottish-Americans, Tommy Armour and Macdonald Smith, who both broke the Interlachen competitive course record.

Missourian Horton Smith became the new leader after the second round with a 70 for 142. Jones was two behind but he had lost a great chance to end the day level with Smith with a disastrous six on the par-four 15th. But that made up for a slice of good fortune on the 9th when he completely mishit his second shot. The ball had no loft and was heading for water but it was travelling fast, hit a lily pad and sped across the water and up the bank to safety, to enable Jones to get his par four when a six or seven was a possibility.

That sort of luck is occasionally needed to win championships, but Jones did not need any such luck in the next round as he played one of his best rounds of the season to shatter the course record with a 68 – his lowest round ever in the Open.

The third and final day saw Jones play two rounds, both with Joe Turnesa. They went out at 9.15 for the start of the record breaking third round and at the turn Jones was on 33, three under par. He returned a

35 for his great score but he could, and should, have returned a 66 had it not been for a stroke lost to par on each of the last two holes.

Jones' great play destroyed all opposition as he built up a five-shot lead over Harry Cooper, but the afternoon round was a complete reversal for Jones – as was often the case when he played morning and afternoon rounds.

The 10,000 fans had come to see Jones win, but he gave them some heart-stopping moments, particularly when he had fives on three of the four short holes to drop six shots. Some breathtaking recovery shots completed a round of 75 that was a mixture of perfection and 24-handicap golf.

Despite playing some 'strange' golf, Jones still enjoyed a lead after the first nine holes, but then started the back nine in 4-5-5-5. That was when Macdonald Smith started to close in, and defeat was a possibility for Jones. His lead was threatened even further when he incurred a two-stroke penalty after going into the lateral water hazard at the 17th, but he came back to show his true grit at the 18th when he holed a 40-foot putt for a birdie three. The putt was over a mound but his famous Calamity Jane putter did the trick. The ball rolled in and the cheering from the gallery – which could be heard for miles around – signified that they felt Jones had done enough to win the third leg of his Grand Slam. They were right. More than 2000 fans waited until dusk for the other competitors to finish, and for the presentation ceremony.

With three legs gone, could Jones now go all the way and complete the 'Impossible Dream.' Only the Merion course and five opponents stood between him and golf's greatest-ever triumph.

Merion had a special place in Bobby Jones' heart as it was on that beautiful Pennsylvania course that he had won his first Amateur Championship. It was now about to witness the culmination of the greatest achievement in the history of golf. Jones' record in the championship was second to none. He had won the title four times between 1924-28 but lost in the first round to Johnny Goodman in 1929 when the tournament became of little significance after his elimination. Despite his good record, Jones faced a quality field including the reigning champion, Harrison Johnston. Never before had one single tournament aroused so much interest, not only in America, but world-wide. After all, Jones was going for the 'Impregnable Quadrilateral' as George Trevor called it.

Jones was full of confidence in practice, and a gallery of 2500 saw him shoot a round of 69 on the final practice day. If ever he was ready for such an occasion, this was it. The course measured a 6565 yard par 70 and Jones had great admiration for it because it was a fair course that rewarded good play.

The first day started with the first 18 holes of a 36-hole stroke-play qualifying competition before going into match-play. Jones made the game look simple and the course easy as he was the only player to break par with a 69. He added a 73 the next day to

head the qualifiers one stroke ahead of George Von Elm, the man who had beaten Jones in the 1926 final at Baltusrol. A new record crowd of 10,000 came to see the final day's qualifying competition.

On the first day of the match-play Jones had to play two rounds, in the morning and afternoon and, as he had shown in Europe, he did not like such demands. Merion was different, however, as he first beat Canadian amateur champion C. Ross Sommerville 5 & 4 in the morning and then beat Sommerville's fellow countryman F.G. Hoblitzel, also 5 & 4, to gain an easy passage into the last eight. Neither Canadian could cope with Jones' brand of play.

The quarter-final was a 36-hole affair against Californian Fay Coleman. Jones struggled to find his form in the morning and only had a half-way lead of two, thanks to winning the final two holes. In the afternoon it was the Jones of old as he broke away to win 6 & 5. But he was clearly showing the pressure of going for the four titles and, had Coleman attacked more, he could have gained a memorable win and ended Jones' quest for the ultimate glory. But it was not to be, and Jones was two steps away from his great achievement.

Jess Sweetser was next to try and topple Jones. Sweetser, from St Louis, had won the British Amateur title in 1926, was a Walker Cup player and had beaten Jones 8 & 7 in the semi-final at Brookline in 1922. If the Grand Slam was in danger, that danger came in the shape of Jess Sweetser. But the huge 15,000 crowd

had nothing to fear – Jones was playing at his best and completely destroyed his opponent, sweeping into a four-hole lead after the first five holes. Although Sweetser came back at him, Jones went into lunch with a four-hole lead and in the second 18 Jones played machine-like golf to win 9 & 8.

So, the final scene was set. The venue: Merion Golf Course. The Date: 27 September 1930. Bobby Jones versus Eugene Homans from Englewood, New Jersey, for the Amateur Championship of the United States of America. But for Jones there was far more at stake – the honor of performing a seemingly impossible feat. The next 36 holes would decide whether it was Eugene Homans – US Champion, or Bobby Jones – legend.

Record crowds once more flocked to Merion, in the hope of being a part of golf history. Eighteen thousand lined the fairways as, hole by hole, Jones built up a big lead. He was out in 39 and three up. But a blistering second nine holes saw him in with a 33 and seven up with 18 to play – victory was in his grasp. Homans showed some resilience in the afternoon but Jones still pulled away to go nine up at one stage. Homans won his third hole of the match at the 27th but two pars meant Jones ran out the 8 & 7 winner.

He had done it – won all four tournaments in the same year – and each and every one of the 18,000 fans wanted to congratulate him. Only bodyguards saved Jones from possible injury in the rush.

Above: Jones (right) with the Walker Cup which his team took back to the United States after a fine 10-2 win. With Jones is the captain of the British team, Roger Wethered, who was to be Jones' opponent in the final of the British Amateur championship a few weeks later.
Above left: A hero's welcome at the railroad station as Jones returns home after winning his first US Open in 1923.

BOBBY JONES' CAREER

His record-breaking four months in 1930 was achieved as follows:

26-31 May	BRITISH AMATEUR CHAMPIONSHIP (St Andrews) Final: beat Roger Wethered 7 & 6
18-20 June	BRITISH OPEN (Hoylake) 291 **Jones** 293 Leo Diegel 293 Macdonald Smith
10-12 July	US OPEN (Interlachen) 287 **Jones** 289 Macdonald Smith 292 Horton Smith
24-27 September	US AMATEUR CHAMPIONSHIP (Merion) Final: beat Eugene Homans 8 & 7

Jones' career record was as follows:

1922	Walker Cup
1923	US Open
1924	US Amateur
	Walker Cup
1925	US Amateur
1926	US Open
	British Open
	Walker Cup
1927	British Open
	US Amateur
1928	US Amateur
	Walker Cup (Capt)
1929	US Open
1930	US Open
	British Open
	US Amateur
	British Amateur
	Walker Cup (Capt)

Findlay S. Douglas, President of the USGA, had the honor of presenting Jones with the winner's trophy. Douglas, like many others, must have been wondering whether this was going to be the final act in Jones' great, but all too short, career. Jones was only 28 at the time of his great achievement and there was talk of him retiring. The media were anxious to know the truth and he announced at Merion that he intended to continue playing. On 17 November, however, H.H. Ramsay, vice-president of the USGA, made an announcement on behalf of Jones saying that the demands of his law practice had forced him to announce his retirement from competitive golf. It was a sad day for the game.

Fortunately the sport did not lose him completely because he made an instructional film for Warner Bros entitled *How I Play Golf* and, of course, the US Masters at Augusta is testament to the great man, as he was responsible for its inauguration in 1934. Jones also played his part in the institution of the Eisenhower Trophy and returned to St Andrews as captain of the American team for the first competition

in 1958. The people of St Andrews gave him the freedom of the burgh, remembering it was at the home of golf that he started out on his march towards winning those four titles 28 years earlier.

The golfing world lost a legend, and a friend, in December 1971 when a crippling illness claimed Jones' life at the age of 69. He died in the knowledge that no man had come close to emulating his feat. It is one of those records that could well last for ever.

BEN HOGAN'S EMOTIONAL WIN

At 8.30 in the morning of 2 February 1949 Ben Hogan and his wife Valerie were travelling to their Fort Worth home in their new Cadillac. They were on their way back from Phoenix where Hogan had been competing in the Phoenix Open, won by Jimmy Demaret.

On an open stretch of road near Van Horn, about 200 miles south of El Paso, Hogan noticed a truck heading toward them in the other lane. Suddenly, a local bus overtook the truck and was heading for the Hogans' car. In an effort to protect his wife, Ben flung himself across her in a moment of bravery. The action not only saved his wife from serious injury but almost certainly saved his own life. The steering wheel he had been sat behind was later found embedded in the back of the driver's seat.

Nevertheless, Hogan still suffered extensive injuries. He lay in agony for one and a half hours before an ambulance arrived, by which time a large gathering of passing motorists had assembled. Stories were soon passed around . . . 'he'll never walk again' . . . 'he'll never play golf again' . . . and some even had it that Hogan was dead.

It was after 1.00 pm when Hogan eventually arrived at El Paso Hospital where it was revealed he had a fractured pelvis, broken collarbone and several minor fractures and other injuries. He spent two months in hospital before returning to his Westover Hills home at Fort Worth on 1 April. He was frail and tired, but still smiling for the fans.

Not only was the golfing world stunned by the accident but the whole of America was devastated. They anxiously waited for reports about improvement in his condition. But not even the most ardent admirer could have believed that the following January he would be up and contesting the Los Angeles Open. But he was. He also figured prominently in the 1950 Masters at Augusta and then, at Merion Golf Club, Ardmore, Pennsylvania, in June that year, he created one of sport's great emotional moments when he won the US Open in only his seventh tournament after his brush with death.

It was the 50th Open and it was appropriate that Merion should be chosen for such an occasion because it was on that course that Bobby Jones had played his first big tournament at the age of 14 and it was also the scene of Jones's final competitive tournament when he completed his 1930 Grand Slam with the Amateur title. It was the first Open at Merion since 1934 when Olin Dutra, a sick man on the final day,

Left: Hogan practicing for the 1950 Los Angeles Open, less than a year after doctors said he would never walk again.
Above: Hogan, playing with Sam Snead, in the 1956 Canada Cup (now World cup) at Wentworth, England.

was last home with a round of 72 for 293 to beat Gene Sarazen by one stroke.

By contrast to 1895 when the first US Open was held, and won by Horace Rawlins who beat off the challenge from 10 other men, the 50th playing saw 165 competitors tee off to try and beat the 6694-yard par-70 East course. Cary Middlecoff, the defending champion, and PGA Champion Sam Snead, who had never won the Open, were two of the favorites. The course suited good drivers, and that was to Snead's advantage. The rough was longer than normal but overall the course was in good condition, albeit tough. But, after all it was the world's toughest tournament to win.

Although Middlecoff and Snead were installed as favorites, Hogan could not be ruled out. Hogan, the 1948 champion, obviously had not defended his title at Medinah in 1949 but he had been playing good golf in the run up to this latest championship. Naturally, there were question marks about Hogan's fitness and in particular about his ability to play 36 holes on the final day. He had not played a tournament that required two rounds in one day since his comeback at Los Angeles. What many people ignored, when talking about his physical state, was Hogan's mental state. He had the desire to win and, if anybody could get the mental approach right, it was Hogan.

On a sun-drenched, but humid, first day, unemployed professional Lee Mackey junior was the sensation, coming home with an Open record 64, beating the 65 set by amateur Jimmy McHale at St Louis in 1947. Even more remarkable, it was Mackey's first Open. The putting from the unknown from Birmingham, Alabama, was some of the best ever seen in the Open. He single putted on 10 greens, and ended his great round with a 12-footer for a birdie three on the 18th. A crowd of 7000 filled the course, but just a handful saw Mackey's record-breaking round. Most eyes were on either Hogan or Snead.

A disappointing outward half 39 by Hogan was bettered by the Texan in the second nine when he returned a 33 for a total of 72. But it was only good putting that saved Hogan, for his driving left a little to be desired. Putts, like the 45-footer for a birdie three at the 12th, helped keep his score down, although he was eight off the lead.

The opening day though really belonged to the unknown golfers. In addition to Mackey, Long Island champion Al Bosch came in with a 67 to take second place, and a new pro of just a couple of months, Julius Boros, needed par at each of the last three holes for a 65, he came in one *over* in each case to finish on 68.

The favorites were put in the shade – which was the best place to be on such a warm day . . . Middle-coff started 3-7-3-6 to go two over after 4 holes, but he recovered for a final 71.

FIRST ROUND LEADERS

64	Lee Mackey, jnr
67	Al Bosch
68	Skip Alexander
68	Julius Boros
69	Harold Williams
69	Henry Williams, jnr

What a difference a day makes . . . ask Lee Mackey and Al Bosch, they will tell you it can make a world of difference. After their championship-leading rounds on day one, they were both 17 shots worse off on day two. Mackey slumped to 81, while Bosch shot an 84 to miss the cut. In the first nine holes Bosch had two sixes and a seven on his card and added another seven on the inward half. At the halfway stage at Medinah the previous year he had been the tournament leader! By contrast to his opening 18 holes, Mackey attracted a large gallery expecting to see more fireworks from the Alabama player. But their hopes were not to be fulfilled.

The day, however, belonged to 'The Arkansas Traveller' – Ernest J (Dutch) Harrison who became the tournament leader on 139 thanks to a fine round of 67. Harrison had started playing golf as a left-hander, but successfully converted to become one of the top right-handed golfers.

The crowd of 10,000 could not keep track of the lead. It changed hands so many times as the previous day's leaders fell away and new men came to prominence. Boros, Australian-born Jim Ferrier, and former pilot Johnny Bulla, who registered the best round of the day, 66, were all just one shot behind Harrison at the end of the day's proceedings. And lurking one

Above: Lloyd Mangrum, who was to finish runner-up to Hogan in the 1950 Open.
Opposite, top: Three studies of perfection, Ben Hogan at work during his recovery from the car accident.
Opposite, bottom: 'Show me the green, I'll hit it' thinks Hogan's great rival Sam Snead.

stroke behind those three was Hogan who came into the picture with a 69.

The field was reduced to 52 for the final day which consisted of 36 holes. Would Hogan's legs last out? That was the question being asked as he faced the toughest battle since that day at Van Horn 16 months earlier. 'He can't do it,' said no less an expert than Gene Sarazen, adding; 'Thirty-six holes in one day will kill him.'

Hogan had been carried this far on a wave of emotion from the American people – there was no way he was going to give in now.

SECOND ROUND LEADERS

139 (72-67)	Dutch Harrison
140 (74-66)	Johnny Bulla
140 (71-69)	Jim Ferrier
140 (68-72)	Julius Boros
141 (72-69)	**Ben Hogan**

Hogan played his final two rounds with one of the pre-tournament favorites, Cary Middlecoff. They teed off at 9.30 for the morning round and at 2.00 in the afternoon. A large part of the 15,000 crowd followed Hogan as the attendance broke the Open record for a single day.

Although Middlecoff had fallen away from the lead, he still played well enough to motivate Hogan who finished the morning round on 72. He was two behind the new tournament leader Lloyd Mangrum who returned a 69 for 211. Jim Ferrier was still in contention, just one behind Hogan on 214.

THIRD ROUND LEADERS

211 (72-70-69)	Lloyd Mangrum
212 (72-67-73)	Dutch Harrison
213 (72-69-72)	**Ben Hogan**
214 (71-69-74)	Jim Ferrier
216 (72-71-73)	Henry Ransom

Above: Hogan practicing his putting before the start of the 1950 Open.
Above left: Julius Boros had plans to upset Hogan's great comeback, but could not sustain the pressure.
Above right: Hogan with the PGA trophy after his 1948 win, his last major success before his victory at Merion.

Scoring in the final 18 holes was again inconsistent and the lead changed hands several times so that the eventual outcome was uncertain until the very last hole.

Any chance Jim Ferrier had disappeared on the first hole as he took seven shots to go from four to seven over par for the tournament. Lloyd Mangrum slipped back on 76 and was in the clubhouse on 287, the same figure as Maryland's George Fazio who returned a final round of 70. Dutch Harrison just failed to join them as his disappointing final round of 76 gave him 288.

With Mangrum and Fazio already home, Hogan knew exactly what he had to do and teeing off at the 15th he was two shots ahead of the pair of them. There

22

BEN HOGAN'S EMOTIONAL WIN

FOURTH ROUND SCOREBOARD

287 (73-72-72-70) George Fazio	
287 (72-69-72-74) **Ben Hogan**	
287 (72-70-69-76) Lloyd Mangrum	
288 (72-67-73-76) Dutch Harrison	
289 (71-69-74-75) Jim Ferrier	
289 (71-74-74-70) Joe Kirkwood, jnr	
289 (72-71-73-73) Henry Ransom	

was a buzz of excitement around the course as most of the gallery focussed on Hogan. None of them believed he could lose the title now. Hogan had stayed calm and played consistently as the others 'blew up' around him. But disaster struck on the 15th green. Hogan three-putted, missing from 18 inches, for a bogey five. He made par at the 16th and just needed two more pars to clinch the title.

At the 230-yard par-three 17th Hogan hit the green with a three iron but the ball rolled off and into the edge of the bunker. He recovered from the sand to within six feet of the pin. His putt was dead on line but stopped short of the hole. It was another bogey, and suddenly he was level with Mangrum and Fazio. Was Hogan going to lose it after all?

He needed a par at the 18th to force a play-off. A birdie was virtually impossible on Merion's toughest par four, measuring 458 yards. Fortunately Ben had no trouble in making par and so he forced a three-way play-off; the first play-off in the Open since 1947 when Lew Worsham beat Sam Snead by one stroke. Hogan, understandably, looked tired at the end of his third day's golf, but he was quick to add that his legs felt fine.

The play-off was over 18 holes and play commenced at 2.00 pm on the Sunday. Ten thousand fans returned to the course to follow the fortunes of the three central characters. Could Hogan complete a remarkable triumph?

Fazio had never come so close to winning a major title before. Would the occasion get the better of him? Mangrum and Hogan had, however, experienced such success. Mangrum had won his first Open, at Canterbury, Cleveland, in 1946, by beating Byron Nelson and Vic Ghezzi in a 36-hole play-off. Hogan's only previous play-off in a major was in the 1942 Masters when he had lost to Byron Nelson by one stroke. But he was determined not to suffer the same fate this time.

After nine holes it was close, Hogan and Mangrum were on 36 and Fazio on 37. But the Maryland player fell away further in the back nine. Hogan improved on Mangrum at the par-four 10th but Mangrum levelled again immediately. Hogan got the one stroke advantage back at 12 and increased it further at the 14th. Mangrum pulled one back at the 15th and then, at the next hole, one of golf's peculiar incidents happened.

Hogan was one up on Mangrum, with Fazio out of the running three behind, Mangrum played a disastrous tee shot but recovered well to get down in what seemed to be a par four. Hogan also made par but Mangrum was penalized two strokes for illegally cleaning his ball when he blew away a bug that had rested on it!

Now leading by three strokes the title was Hogan's. He confirmed it with a birdie two at the 17th and finished with his par for a 69.

The crowd, which had willed Hogan on for four days, went wild. The man they said would never play again defied all the odds in one of the greatest-ever sporting comebacks.

PLAY-OFF: HOLE-BY-HOLE

Hole	1	2	3	4	5	6	7	8	9		10	11	12	13	14	15	16	17	18		Par
Par	4	5	3	5	4	4	4	4	3	36	4	4	4	3	4	4	4	3	4	34	70
Hogan	4	5	3	5	4	4	3	5	3	36	4	4	4	3	4	4	4	2	4	33	69
Mangrum	4	4	4	5	4	4	4	4	3	36	5	3	5	3	5	3	6	3	4	37	73
Fazio	5	4	3	5	4	5	5	3	3	37	4	4	4	3	5	5	5	3	5	38	75

ARNIE'S CHARGE

When 26-year-old Arnold Palmer joined the US Tour in 1955 he arrived on the professional scene like a breath of fresh air. The professional game had gone into decline in the United States and Britain and, with Ben Hogan heading for retirement, golf was looking for its next 'superstar' and that is where Palmer stepped in.

Born at Latrobe, Pennsylvania, in 1929, Palmer, the son of a steelworker, gave notice of his arrival when he beat Robert Sweeny by one hole to win the 1954 US Amateur title at Detroit. He turned professional shortly after and in 1958 Palmer was leading money winner on the US Tour thanks to wins in the St Petersburg Open, Pepsi Golf tournament, and his first major – the Masters.

Suddenly people who had never dreamed of playing golf were interested by this one man alone. He had taken the sport to the masses and they responded by filling golf courses up and down the United States. He also helped re-stimulate enthusiasm among many professional golfers and Palmer was instrumental in getting his fellow Americans to make the annual pilgrimage across the Atlantic to play in the British Open. Interest in the British Open among American players had waned considerably but Palmer knew the British Open was too great to be shunned and he was responsible for a great many of his compatriots going to St Andrews for the Centenary Open in 1960. Palmer lost by one stroke to Australian Kel Nagle but he had succeeded in getting his fellow professionals to compete. The rest is history as American golfers have virtually monopolized the event in the 25 years since Palmer's arrival.

The British fans idolized Palmer in the same way as the American fans did and he soon established his famous 'Arnie's Army' on both sides of the Atlantic.

When Palmer arrived at St Andrews in 1960, in search of his third consecutive major he had, the previous month, added the US Open to the Masters he had won earlier in the year. His victory in the US Open provided golf with one of those truly great moments as he had recovered from seven shots off the lead at the start of the final round to win the title by two strokes.

It was Palmer's third US Open. He had finished equal 23rd in 1958 and equal 5th in 1959. Was he ready to win the title in 1960? His vast army of fans had no doubt – he was.

The beautiful setting of the Cherry Hills Country Club near Denver was chosen as the venue for the 60th US Open and it was the second time the Colora-

Left: Palmer looking more like an angler . . . at Portmarnock, Ireland in 1960.
Right: It may only be a practice session, but the determination is the same.
Below: 1960 was a good year for Palmer, since he was also a member (with Sam Snead, right) of the winning Canada Cup team.
Bottom: Typical Palmer action, at Augusta in 1960 when he won his second Masters title.

do course had hosted the championship. The only other occasion was in 1938 when Ralph Guldahl won for the second successive year. The 130 starters had to contend with the rarified atmosphere of the Cherry Hills course, set one mile above sea level, which was expected to help keep scores low, but don't mention low scores to Ray Ainsley. It was during the 1938 Open at Cherry Hills that Ainsley created an Open record by taking 19 strokes at one hole – the par-four 16th. His ball landed in the creek adjacent to the fairway and, as he took shot-after-shot to try and remove his ball, without success, a little girl watching turned to her mother and said, after he did eventually get it out: 'It must be dead now mummy, that man's stopped swinging his stick at it!'

The snow-capped Rocky Mountains in the background made the setting attractive but many golfers who arrived for the 1960 Championship felt the 7004-yard par-71 course was too easy for such a major event and many par-4 greens were capable of being driven because of the thin air. One competitor, 20-year-old amateur Jack Nicklaus, actually hit the 548-yard par-five 17th green in two, using a seven iron for his second shot!

But all eyes were on Palmer as his fans wanted to see him emulate Craig Wood and Ben Hogan and win the Masters and Open in one year. The record first-day gallery of nearly 14,000 seemed to be divided into two halves – Arnie's fans, and 'the rest.'

The first-day crowd witnessed an unusual day's golf to say the least. Mike Souchak attacked the course for an outward 31 before finishing on 68. But 1958 champion Tommy Bolt was one of the few golfers who had difficulty. He returned an 80 including one hole where he angrily threw his driver into a lake into which he had just driven twice. The club just missed playing partner Claude Harmon and Bolt was so annoyed he withdrew himself from the tournament. His actions resulted in a $100 fine imposed by the PGA. That same lake, at the 18th, also posed a problem for Doug Sanders. Just as he was about to drive a fish leaped from the water and landed on the fairway in front of him. The gymnastic vertebrate was returned to its domain, but when Sanders eventually got his tee shot away, his ball followed the fish into the lake! He was well in contention on 3-under at the time and the fish cost him two strokes. If he was to lose the Championship, how could he forget that creature for the rest of his life?

It was a bizarre day also for the new folk-hero Palmer. He drove into the creek at the first hole and could have been in big trouble had a young boy not pulled the ball out of the water. PGA officials decided that Palmer should drop the ball for a one-stroke penalty, an easier option than playing out of the creek. Palmer finished the day on 72, four behind the leader Souchak.

Souchak again destroyed the course in the second round with eight 3s in his total of 67 which created a new Open record of 135 for the first 36 holes. Doug Sanders went second, three behind Souchak. There were no fish for Sanders at the 18th this time – he made a birdie three to complete his round in 68. While Palmer was attracting his usual high percentage of the 14,751 crowd, 47-year-old Ben Hogan, attempting to win his fifth Open, stole a lot of Palmer's limelight when he returned a 67 for his lowest round since his great win in 1953.

The greens had been watered overnight and that

26

was expected to favor Palmer. He went round the first nine holes in 34 and one of his famous charges was expected on the inward nine but it did not materialize as he covered the second nine in 37 for 143, eight strokes off the lead. His deficit could have been more had it not been for some luck at the 14th.

Palmer played the par-four hole like an amateur. He was out of bounds with his drive, then pulled his second drive into the bank of the creek. He recovered to within 30-feet of the pin and holed for a five, just one over par, when he could not have complained if he had made six or seven. It was Palmer's style of play, just like this, that helped the ordinary golfer identify with him. That was part of the great man's appeal, but those who imitated his style could only dream of being as great as Palmer himself.

Opposite page: A young Arnold Palmer with one of the first 'Arnie's Armies.'
Left: Palmer followed up his 1960 US Open success with victory in the British Open at Royal Birkdale the following year. He won again at Troon in 1962.
Below: Jack Nicklaus, then an amateur, engaged in a great battle with Palmer at Cherry Hills.

Although Palmer had his own vast army of fans, Hogan was stealing part of the limelight and so too was Jack Nicklaus. Nicklaus had been 1959 US Amateur champion and this was his second US Open. He had finished joint 41st at Southern Hills in 1958 but now he was attracting a lot of interest and being talked about as the first amateur winner since Johnny Goodman 27 years earlier. Nicklaus was one ahead of Palmer at the end of the second round, in itself a remarkable feat for the youngster.

Mike Souchak managed to hold on to his lead at the end of the third round but a six at the 18th meant he only led Jerry Barber, Dow Finsterwald and Julius Boros by two. An amateur cameraman put Souchak off at the last hole, and he was visibly angry at the actions of the young man. Following close behind the first four were Ben Hogan and Jack Nicklaus who both returned 69s for three round totals of 211 but 'Arnie's Army' must have felt he was out of the race as he was

seven behind Souchak on 215. But the afternoon's concluding 18 holes brought about one of the game's great transformations and recoveries.

Palmer has since proved in his long career that he is never one to give up, and he has always shown a desire to attack. That is just what he did to Souchak's seemingly impregnable lead on Saturday 18 June 1960.

The man from Latrobe equalled Jimmy McHale's Open record with a 30 on the first nine holes, having started the round with four consecutive birdie 3s. As Palmer moved up the leader board, so too did Hogan and Nicklaus, who were playing together; but Souchak made the opposite journey down the leader board and completed his final round in 75, four over par.

When Souchak reached the tenth he was on 244 with Jack Fleck. Hogan, Palmer and Boros were one behind but the new leader was Nicklaus on 243. The

Below: The style that made Arnold Palmer the great champion that he was, and for so long.

blond-haired amateur from Ohio had done enough to have himself compared with the great Bobby Jones. Even if he did not go on to win the title, Cherry Hills had been lucky to see the birth of a new star.

But, there was still a lot of golf left in Cherry Hills.

Poor old Doug Sanders, remember, he was the guy with the fishy problem on day one: he started the final day in second place but ended the tournament in 46th place after final-round totals of 82 and 77 – so that mysterious fish did not play its part in the drama of the 1960 US Open after all. The 47-year-old Texan Ben Hogan nearly did, but he could not produce another of his emotional triumphs as a six and seven at the last two holes cost him dearly. Nicklaus was playing well and it was down to him to provide the challenge to the marauding Palmer as Souchak fell away.

Palmer played some of the most consistent golf of his career and his final 18 holes contained no fewer than seven birdies. It was that consistency that saw him go past Nicklaus with a round of 65 to beat the man from Columbus by two strokes. Palmer, once

more, was favored by a piece of good fortune when he chipped in from 30 feet at the 2nd for a birdie three, but the remainder of his round can only be described as sheer genius.

Arnold Palmer came back from seven behind in one of the greatest recoveries in championship golf. That was to be his only US Open triumph and, ironically, six years later he led Billy Casper by seven strokes with nine holes to play – and *lost*. But Palmer's contribution to the game of golf is measured, not by the number of trophies he has won, but by his attitude.

He proved to the masses it could be fun as he made the game look easy and relaxed. He also made other professionals more aware of the game and he helped them considerably by bringing big money into the sport, and for that reason players and spectators alike have to be grateful to Palmer. Those who were at Cherry Hills on the June day in 1960 will never forget his great charge as he won the world's toughest golf tournament.

Left: Things weren't always rosy for Palmer as his face tells its own story during the 1966 Masters.
Below: Doug Sanders certainly had a fisherman's tale to tell when he got to the 19th!

1960 US OPEN STATISTICS

FIRST ROUND LEADERS

68	Mike Souchak
69	Jerry Barber
69	Henry Ransom

SECOND ROUND LEADERS

135	Mike Souchak	68-67
138	Doug Sanders	70-68
140	Dow Finsterwald	71-69
140	Jerry Barber	69-71
140	Jack Fleck	70-70

THIRD ROUND LEADERS

208	Mike Souchak	68-67-73
210	Jerry Barber	69-71-70
210	Dow Finsterwald	71-69-70
210	Julius Boros	73-69-68
211	Ben Hogan	75-67-69
211	Jack Nicklaus	71-71-69
(215	**Arnold Palmer**	72-71-72)

FINAL SCORES

280	**Arnold Palmer**	72-71-72-65
282	Jack Nicklaus	71-71-69-71
283	Dutch Harrison	74-70-70-69
283	Julius Boros	73-69-68-73
283	Mike Souchak	68-67-73-75
283	Dow Finsterwald	71-69-70-73
283	Jack Fleck	70-70-72-71
283	Ted Kroll	72-69-75-67

Palmer never won the US Open again but came second (or tied second) on the following occasions:

1962   Oakmont (lost play-off 71-74 to Jack Nicklaus)
1963   Brookline (lost three-way play-off, third behind Julius Boros, 70, and Jacky Cupit, 73. Palmer had 76)
1966   Olympic Club (lost play-off 69-73 to Billy Casper)
1967   Baltusrol (second to Nicklaus, four shots behind).

Above left: A lot older, a lot wiser, but still loving every minute of it. Arnie sees a putt drop in during a 1985 tournament. Arnie still competes regularly on the Seniors' circuit.
Left: Cherry Hills had a commemorative plaque laid to mark Palmer's great achievement – so did Royal Birkdale after his Open win the following year. No golfer has commanded such an honor before, or since then.

LEE TREVINO'S AMAZING 20 DAYS

Lee Trevino has a reputation for constantly upstaging his fellow players in the joke stakes but in the 20 days between 21 June and 10 July 1971 he also upstaged them in one of the greatest golfing trebles ever achieved.

Only the great Scottish-American Tommy Armour had won the Canadian and US Open titles in the same year (1927) and only Bobby Jones, Ben Hogan and Gene Sarazen had won the British and US Opens in one year but no man had won all three until those days in 1971.

In his four years on the US Tour 'Supermex' had rapidly risen to become the top money winner in 1970 with over $157,000 to his credit, although his only 1970 Tour wins were in the Tucson and National Airlines tournaments. In his build-up to the first leg of his treble, the Open at Merion, Trevino had been playing very consistent golf and had won the Tallahassee Open and Danny Thomas Memphis Classic. Understandably he was installed as one of the pre-Open favorites along with Jack Nicklaus who was returning to the Merion course that had fond memories for him. It was at this beautiful Pennsylvania course that Nicklaus had inspired the United States team to a record 42-stroke victory in the 1960 Eisenhower Trophy when, as a 20-year-old, he had four rounds all under 69.

Merion, which first staged the Open in 1934 when Olin Dutra beat Gene Sarazen by one stroke, has also been the scene of many great golfing moments: like Bobby Jones completing his Grand Slam in 1930 and Ben Hogan winning the 1950 Open shortly after his bad accident. But now it was 31-year-old Trevino's turn to provide his own piece of record-breaking magic on the famous course.

A week before the Open, Trevino had lost a four-man play-off in the Kemper Open won by Tom Weiskopf, who ended a barren three-year spell without a Tour win. Trevino could have won the title outright had he birdied the 72nd hole instead of making par. Weiskopf, now that he had returned to winning ways, was another obvious threat and still around was Arnold Palmer, competing in his 12th Open.

A 21-year-old student, Lanny Wadkins, took the final practice session by storm when he had a five-under-par 29 on the inward nine but, although he could not match Wadkins' scoring, Trevino was not to be left out of the limelight. After hitting a wayward shot into deep rough he was seen to emerge with a snake wrapped around his club. Any fears were soon

dispelled when it was revealed the joker had carried a rubber replica in his bag for such an occasion.

Merion, with its distinctive wicker baskets on top of the pins instead of flags, was chosen for its record 13th USGA Championship and its distance of just over 6500 yards was the shortest for a post-war Open. But it still offered its usual amount of treachery and Billy Casper said: 'You don't need a course to be over 7000 yards for it to be a good one.' Merion was short but its fairways, weaving through the dogwood and evergreens, made it demanding while the thicker-than-usual rough made accurate driving essential as some fairways were only 30 yards wide. It was described as a thinking man's course and accurate use of all clubs, not only the driver, was called for.

Defending champion Tony Jacklin started the 1971 championship with an eagle two at the second and looked like carrying on where he left off at Hazeltine, but he fell away for a five-over 75. Trevino, after a bad opening nine holes in 37, came home in 33 for a par 70. But two former amateur champions stole the first-day limelight, even upstaging Trevino.

The 1970 amateur champion Lanny Wadkins shot a 68 while 1962 National Amateur champion Labron Harris junior shot an amazing 67 for the outright lead. Harris, from Stillwater, Oklahoma, broke 70 in the Open for the first time, at his ninth attempt. Doug Sanders and Bob Goalby joined Wadkins on 68 while Nicklaus was not far away on 69. It was going to be quite a tournament.

Left: The killer punch . . . a birdie at the 12th in the play-off and Nicklaus' hopes of winning the US Open for the third time had gone.
Below: Mr Lu can't even watch as Trevino throws his ball to the gallery after clinching the British Open.

Jack Nicklaus and Arnold Palmer criticized the playing conditions on the second day and, if those two stalwarts complain, something must be amiss. Nicklaus felt the pin placements were all wrong while Palmer's complaint was about the slowness of play.

The surprise co-leaders at the end of day two were Jim Colbert and Bob Erickson who had just one Tour win between them – Colbert's 1969 Monsanto Open win. But Colbert added a second successive 69 while Erickson shot a great 67 to go with his first day's 71 to give them both 138. Trevino shot a 72 for 142 and four off the lead. Defending-champion Jacklin missed the cut, the sixth defending champion in nine years to drop out at the half-way stage.

Twenty-one year old Wake Forest college junior Jim Simons swept into the lead on the third day in one of golf's great fairy tales. The amateur's 65 put him on 207, two ahead of Jack Nicklaus, and equalled Jimmy McHale's 1947 record low by an amateur in the Open when he also shot a 65, at St Louis. Simons became the first amateur since Marty Flackman in 1967 to

Trevino settled down earlier than Nicklaus and went two up after three holes. Nicklaus then got into it and pulled one back before the half-way mark when play was held up for 35 minutes because of a lightning storm. After that Nicklaus let it slip and two erratic bunker shots were the key to the eventual outcome as Trevino strung together two birdies and seven pars on the inward nine for still another 33 which was good enough to give him the title by three strokes in the first play-off in the Open since Billy Casper beat Arnold Palmer by four strokes at the Olympic Club, California, in 1966.

With the first leg of his treble successfully won, Trevino's next task was the Canadian Open and he set off north of the border with the band of fans he had nicknamed 'Lee's Fleas.' After all, Arnie had his Army, why couldn't Lee have his Fleas?

Montreal's Richelieu Valley course was packed with 12,000 Canadian fans who came to watch the cream of the American professionals for the 62nd Canadian Open, but they were also hoping for the first 'home' win since Pat Fletcher had won the title in 1954. The five-year-old course was overshadowed by cloudy skies on the opening day as Trevino covered the 6920-yard course in 73 thanks to birdies on the last two holes after earlier disasters in which he three-putted three of the greens. French-speaking Canadians were prominent among the crowd and officials, and Trevino enjoyed the occasional banter with them in his limited French tongue, much to the crowd's delight, but he could not satisfy the fans with a share of the four-man lead which belonged to Rolf Deming, an ex-University of Minnesota mathematics teacher, Lou Graham, Rod Funseth and Phil Rodgers.

However, they were all upstaged by a 47-year-old on the second day as Art Wall junior showed his younger counterparts how the game should be played with a round of calm, calculated golf, without the risks which many of the younger players were taking. Wall had won the 1959 Masters when he pulled back six strokes in the final round to beat Stan Leonard and Arnold Palmer and had also won the Canadian title in 1960 and so was looking for a double. Trevino, meanwhile, was hoping for the second leg of his even rarer treble. Supermex shot a 68 to give him 141, four strokes behind the new leader. Trevino was, perhaps, a little fortunate to play in the morning on the second day, as strong winds dried out the greens rapidly after lunch and made scoring high. But weather conditions often seem immaterial to Trevino as he delights the gallery with his spontaneous wit and humor and he did just that with the large portion of the 12,000 crowd that followed his round.

lead the Open at the end of 54 holes. Could he become the first amateur for nearly 40 years to win the title? With Nicklaus just two behind and Trevino coming into form thanks to a third round 69 life was going to be tough for the youngster on the final day.

Simons had played his third round with Trevino and admitted that Lee's relaxed style and constant joking helped him relax himself. It did not do Trevino any harm either as his 69, thanks to another great back nine of 33, kept him in contention. Simons did not have the benefit of playing with Trevino on the final day and he allowed the pressure to get to him, returning a 76 for a four-round total of 283 and a share of fifth place, thus missing out on being the first amateur since Johnny Goodman in 1933 to win the title. But, as the youngster slipped away it left the door open for Nicklaus and Trevino to fight out the Championship.

At one stage it looked as though Nicklaus was going to have it all to himself but Trevino put in yet another of his famous back-nine sprints and returned a 33 once more. He could have assured himself of the title with a par on the 18th, but bogeyed it instead. Minutes later Nicklaus reached the 18th and had a 12-foot putt for a birdie, and the title. But he missed, the two were tied on 280 and they had to come back the next day to do battle over 18 extra holes.

Above left: Mr Lu, the man who won over many admirers at Birkdale.
Above right: It was this sort of determination that took Trevino to his three titles within 21 days.
Right: The large crowd at Birkdale were treated to one of the best ever finishes in a British Open.

The wisecracking continued all the way round on the third day when Trevino attracted another big following. This time he was paired with local hero, French-speaking Adrian Bigras and the crowd thought the pairing was terrific. They were, however, divided because they had adopted Trevino as their favorite, but in their hearts would dearly have loved to see a local man win his national title. But it was Trevino who won their individual battle with a great 67 and moved to within two shots of Wall who clung on to his lead with a 69 – the first time since the 1966 Hartford Open that Wall had led a tournament after 54 holes. Trevino's mastering of the par 3s, on which he had three deuces and one par, was an important factor in his 67.

Wall looked like holding on to his lead as he still led by two at the end of 63 holes, despite Trevino's eagle two at the first hole. But, once more, Trevino stormed through the last nine holes in 33, which was fast becoming his trademark, to put together three birdies to Wall's one and force a tie. The play-off was sudden death and the first hole was the 410-yard 15th, chosen to accommodate the television cameras. Tre-

vino drove to the edge of the rough, chipped to within 18 feet with a wedge and sank his birdie putt to win at the first extra hole. Wall was devastated, no doubt recalling the 1967 Canadian Open when he had lost the sudden-death play-off to Billy Casper.

Trevino had become only the second man, after Tommy Armour in 1927, to win both Canadian and US Opens in the same year. He left the Montreal course immediately to catch a plane for England where he was hoping to become the first man to add the British Open to that list. His parting shot to the Canadian people was: 'Tell England Supermex is on his way.'

For winning the Canadian title Trevino picked up another $30,000, taking his season's winnings to near the $200,000 mark, by far the biggest winner on the US Tour in 1971. But that counts for nothing when faced with a course like that of Royal Birkdale – you cannot buy your way round the tough Lancashire seaside links. Skill is the only criterion when playing one of Britain's toughest courses.

The mountainous sand dunes, hills, humps, and raging wind off the Irish Sea call for the best out of any

Far left: The 1970 amateur champion Lanny Wadkins shot an opening 68 in the US Open after an inward nine of 29 during the practice round the day before.
Left: Amateur Jim Simons shot a 65 to go two ahead of Jack Nicklaus in the third round of the US Open at Merion.
Above: Great rivals, but also great friends, Nicklaus and Trevino.

player, whether it be in the Open or a local Sunday morning medal. Many of the leading players arrived and were surprised at the slowness of the greens, particularly Bob Charles and, as one of the world's leading putters, he was well qualified to make such a comment. While Trevino was enjoying his success in Montreal a storm had flooded the Southport course, and heavier-than-usual June rains had made the greens slower, but the weather made little difference to the severity of the fairways, lined with their usual devilish array of willow scrub.

Despite Trevino's great run of success, in which he had not finished out of the first ten in 11 straight tournaments, Jack Nicklaus was installed as the favorite for the 100th British Open. The 'Golden Bear' came to Birkdale via Wimbledon where he had enjoyed a relaxing few days watching John Newcombe beat Stan Smith to win the mens' title.

This was Birkdale's fourth British Open since Australian Peter Thomson first won over the course in 1954. Arnold Palmer won his first British Open at Birkdale in 1961 and Thomson won again in 1965. Palmer was not present this time, having pulled out after a poor showing in the Canadian Open. But, by the law of averages it was America's turn to provide another winner, and there were plenty who had made the trip in an effort to try and get their name engraved on the famous claret jug.

England's own hero, the 1969 winner Tony Jacklin, enjoyed a share of the first-day lead on 69 with Argentinian Vicente Fernandez, Howie Johnson from Minnesota, who had the lead for most of the day, and Trevino who, for a change, had a better outward nine (33) than inward nine (36). Trevino's putting was magic, and he had nine single putts and only one three putt all day. He had six birdies in his first round, four of them on the relatively easy par fives. It was those par fives, however, that cost Jack Nicklaus a share of the championship lead.

Nicklaus started the day in blistering fashion, going four under after just four holes, and completed the first nine in 32. He continued to play steady golf on the inward nine but then had sixes at the last two holes, both par fives, for a 71, two strokes off the lead.

Trevino reverted to his back nine charge on the second day when he added a 33 to his outward 37 thanks to a 40-foot putt for an eagle three at the 18th, giving him a total of 139 and a share of the lead. He had started disastrously with three bogeys in a row in his first nine for that 37 but, as the sun came out in the early evening, it was as if the inspiration he had been looking for had finally arrived, and he charged to a five-under-par total.

Tony Jacklin shared the lead with Trevino and the pair of them were one stroke ahead of Taiwan's Liang Huan Lu – known affectionately as 'Mr Lu,' who shot a second successive 70 which put him just one behind the joint leaders.

Trevino became outright leader after his third-round 69, one stroke ahead of Jacklin, who continued to delight his own loyal fans, and Mr Lu, who shot a 69. Those two were then three ahead of Gary Player and American-born Briton Craig de Foy.

Again, it was the last nine that carried Trevino through. Like the previous day he had three consecutive bogeys in the first nine, but then had six birdies in the back nine to keep him in the lead. However, the new hero was undoubtedly the little Taiwanese golfer who was delighting the 17,000-plus fans with his golf, and manners. Permanently wearing a trilby, he would doff it to acknowledge the crowd's cheers and applause. His presence was like a breath of fresh air and, whether he went on to win the title or not, the name of Mr Lu was firmly embedded on the hearts of all those who saw him at Birkdale.

As it was, it turned out not to be Lu's championship, but how close he came to taking the title from Trevino. Playing with Trevino on the final day he was powerless as the American single putted the first six greens and had four birdies for a nine-hole total of 31 and a five-stroke lead over Lu. The likeable Oriental had played consistent golf while the other challenger, Jacklin, slipped away in the opening nine holes. With such a big lead and the usually reliable back nine facing Trevino, there were few of the record crowd for an Open in England, who would have put money against Trevino. But the inward nine nearly turned the whole Open upside-down.

Above: If Trevino was not going to be the British Open winner at Birkdale then the fans would dearly have loved Liang Huan Lu, 'Mr Lu,' to have taken the title.
Above left: Trevino with the coveted US Open trophy . . . and
Below left: Playing at Augusta in the Masters, one trophy he has still to win.
Below: Home favorite Tony Jacklin was also in contention at Birkdale.

Tony Jacklin made a come-back while Lu continued to play consistent golf. With two holes still to play Trevino was three up on Lu and four up on Jacklin, defeat was still impossible to imagine, but then disaster struck at the 17th.

Trevino's drive did not have the expected fade on it and headed straight for sand where it was buried. His first attempt to get out was abortive. When he did get out of the trap his shot went across the fairway into deep rough on the right. He made a great recovery with a chip shot to within 12 feet of the pin but then three putted for a seven. Mr Lu was home in par and Trevino's lead was cut to one. But any chances the Taiwanese golfer had of winning disappeared at the 18th when his drive landed close to the edge of a bunker leaving him a difficult second shot. Trevino put the disaster at the 17th behind him to come home with a birdie four. Lu made his birdie as well but it was to no avail, Trevino was the British Open champion by one stroke. He fell to the green after sinking his winning putt and buried his face in his hands to hide his emotions. It had been a hard-fought victory but it had been the end to one of the greatest 20-day periods in the history of professional golf. Trevino had become the first, and only man, to win the Open championship of the United States, Canada, and Great Britain in the same year.

A week after his triumph at Birkdale Trevino was back in action in the Western Open: he finished joint 32nd and picked up just $870.

US OPEN
17-21 June 1971
Merion Golf Club, Pennsylvania
280 **Lee Trevino** 70-72-69-69
280 Jack Nicklaus 69-72-68-71
(Play-off: Trevino 68, Nicklaus 71)
282 Bob Rosburg 71-72-70-69
282 Jim Colbert 69-69-73-71

CANADIAN OPEN
1-4 July 1971
Richelieu Valley, Montreal
275 **Lee Trevino** 73-68-67-67
275 Art Wall, Jnr 70-67-69-69
(Play-off: Trevino won at 1st extra hole)
281 Phil Rodgers 67-72-73-69

BRITISH OPEN
7-10 July, 1971
Royal Birkdale
278 **Lee Trevino** 69-70-69-70
279 Liang Huan Lu 70-70-69-70
280 Tony Jacklin 69-70-70-71
281 Craig de Foy 72-72-68-69

THE BEST MASTERS OF ALL

The Augusta National Golf Course was the brain-child of the legendary Bobby Jones. It was founded in 1931, the year after Jones announced his retirement from competitive golf, and he chose Augusta as the site for his course because it was his wife's home town. The course was designed with the help of leading Scottish architect Dr Alistair Mackenzie and the results of their work are there for all to see today as Augusta displays all the beauty nature can offer.

Three years after the course's opening Jones instituted the Masters – an invitation event, with a top-class field. Today, it remains as prestigious as ever as players seek to add their name to the list of greats who have worn the famous green jacket that goes to the winner, as well as having that name engraved alongside such notables as Gene Sarazen, Ben Hogan, Byron Nelson, Sam Snead, Arnold Palmer, Gary Player and, of course, Jack Nicklaus on the famous trophy.

Nicklaus has been involved in many great golf climaxes during his long career, and he has played some of his finest golf at the great Augusta course, but his victory in the 1975 Masters provided one of the finest finishes ever seen in the great tournament as he won the coveted trophy for a record fifth time. While Tom Weiskopf and Johnny Miller played their part in a great finish, they could not upstage the Masters' 'Master', Nicklaus.

Pre-Masters publicity had a new dimension in 1975 as it marked a significant breakthrough for black golfers with Lee Elder becoming the first black player to compete in the great tournament. Elder was the center of publicity as he fulfilled a life-long dream to play in the Masters. Aged 40 at the time, he had been on the US Tour since 1968 and had, in fact, qualified for the Masters 51 weeks earlier when he won the Monsanto Open at Pensacola. Elder's presence caused as much media interest as the first event in 1934 when there had been talk of Bobby Jones coming out of retirement. When Elder stepped out as one of the 15 first-timers he certainly knew what Jack Nicklaus meant when he described the Masters as: 'A monument to everything that is great in golf.'

The field of 76 was filled with its usual host of champions, past and present, and there was no more welcome player than Slammin' Sam himself – Sam Snead – who was playing in his 36th consecutive Masters. He had not missed one since first competing in 1937.

But nostalgia counts for nothing at Augusta as

Above: Jack Nicklaus (left) and Gary Player have won eight Masters titles between them.
Above right: Tom Weiskopf doesn't mind the rain after winning the 1973 British Open. But there was no such luck for him at Augusta in 1975 – he finished runner-up for the fourth time.
Right, bottom: Jack Nicklaus, determination and concentration at their best.

man tries to beat the course. And if one man could beat it then four-times winner Jack Nicklaus could. He had already won the Doral Eastern Open and Heritage Classic that season and was in top form. But Nicklaus was meeting opposition from the new wonder boy of golf, 27-year-old Johnny Miller. Miller had won seven Tour events in 1974 and topped the money list. He also had won one major during his four years on the Tour – the 1973 US Open. Lee Trevino had never fared well in the Masters; in fact he had never finished in the first three, but he, like Nicklaus, was having a good season and could not be ignored. From the outsiders, Tom Weiskopf was the pick of the bunch. Three times runner-up in the Masters, he was hoping to make it 'fourth-time lucky' and victory in the Greater Greensboro Open the week before the Masters certainly boosted his confidence.

As Nicklaus prepared to win the 39th championship and become the first man to don the famous green jacket a fifth time, he must have put fear into his opponents when he said he was better prepared for this than any of his other Masters appearances. The

Above: Bobby Nichols led the field on the first day of the 1975 Masters with a 67.
Right: Three great golfers, Tony Jacklin (left), Tom Weiskopf (driving), and Bert Yancey (watching) . . . none of them won a Masters title, however.

course was meticulously prepared as usual, and the par-72, 7020-yard layout demanded its usual high standard of accuracy.

Nicklaus went out on the first day with amateur Curtis Strange who, like all amateurs, had, by tradition, the honor of playing with a former Masters champion. As a result of some rain the greens were slow and there were 14 sub-par rounds on the opening day. The first-day leader was not any of the big names but 39-year-old Bobby Nichols from Louisville, Kentucky.

Nichols had been on the Tour 15 years but this was to be his finest hour as he astounded the crowd, and himself, with a first-round 67, one ahead of Nicklaus. The 'Golden Bear' was tied on 68 with Miller – not Johnny, but Allen, a fifth-year pro, who has had to live with the tag of 'The Other Miller.' The 'real' Miller shot a miserable three-over-par 75, but that

gave no indication as to what fireworks he had up his sleeve for the final two rounds.

Breathing down the leader's necks was none other than Arnie Palmer whose 69 was his best opening round since 1964 when he had last won the title. Could he do it again? No, surely not!

Weiskopf shot himself into contention with a 69 and who should be there on 71 but Sam Snead – the 'Geriatric Wonder' as the *New York Times* described him. The much publicized Lee Elder disappointed with a 74 and thus deprived the press of their lead story.

Bobby Nichols' moment of glory was soon forgotten on day two as Jack Nicklaus hammered the course with a blistering 67 to build up a five-stroke lead, equalling Herman Keiser's lead at the half way stage in 1946. Nicklaus gave a one-man exhibition of golf at the highest level. But, as talk of 'who'll be runner-up?' was beginning, Nicklaus was quick to point out that he had seen five-shot leads whittled away – it had even happened to him. But quite when, nobody could remember. Nicklaus had six birdies in his great round, including three in succession at the 'Amen Corner' (11th-12th-13th) where many Masters have been won or lost in the past. His only mistake of the day was missing the green with his 3-iron second shot at the 18th for a bogey five.

For a moment the great army of Arnold Palmer fans had plenty to cheer when he had held the lead at five under after nine holes but even Arnie could do nothing as Nicklaus started his charge with his successive birdies. Lee Elder left the competition without the glare of publicity under which he entered it and Sam Snead also went out but, unlike Elder, he made the cut for the third round, only a muscle injury preventing him from carrying on. Bobby Nichols fell back to a six-man group on 141 which included Tom Weiskopf. Johnny Miller, who was to share the stage with Nicklaus and Weiskopf on the final day, had a 71 for 146 – fully 11 strokes behind Nicklaus.

When Jack Nicklaus said: 'Even I drop five-shot leads,' he surely was not serious. But he tempted fate by saying it and, lo and behold, at the end of the third round he was lying second by one stroke to Tom Weiskopf.

Nicklaus played his round with Arnold Palmer and they have a record of playing badly when paired together. This was certainly one of the occasions when neither could have done with playing badly – but they both did: Nicklaus losing the lead after a 73 and Palmer moving out of contention after a 75.

Tom Weiskopf, Nicklaus's old college pal, took the lead with a faultless 66 for a three-round total of 207, overtaking Nicklaus with a 15-foot birdie putt at the 18th. But the day belonged to Johnny Miller whose 65 was just one off the Masters' record. He did, however, create another record, with six consecutive birdies between the second and seventh holes to beat the record of five established a year earlier by Hale Irwin and Gary Player. Miller's 65 put him four behind Weiskopf. One stroke behind Miller was Tom Watson, searching for his first major.

The fourth and final day was to provide one of the most exciting finishes ever seen on a golf course, and proceedings were orchestrated, of course, by Jack Nicklaus. Nicklaus and Augusta are like the proverbial strawberries and cream – they both need each other. And Big Jack was not going to let his third-round disaster put him off. This was his tournament and he was going to get back into it.

Low scoring was the order of the final day and Hale Irwin gained some consolation for losing his

Above: Nicklaus watches the 'Young Pretender,' Tom Watson, drive during the 1975 Masters.
Above left: Johnny Miller shared second place at Augusta but had his day in the British Open in 1976.
Below left: Winning is still a nice feeling, as Jack's expression shows after his fourth PGA win in 1975.
Below: Nicklaus celebrates his decisive birdie at the 16th.

'birdie' record to Miller the previous day by equalling the Augusta record with a 64 to put him at the head of 'also-rans' along with first-day leader Bobby Nichols.

Miller showed no respect for the course again as he returned a 66 for a final total of 277. His final 36 holes created a new Masters record, as did his final 54-hole total of 202.

The scoring does not tell the whole story of the exciting climax to a great tournament.

Nicklaus and Weiskopf kept exchanging the lead. Three times it changed, and twice they were level over the final round. Nicklaus was playing ahead of the other two who were playing together. As Nicklaus approached the 16th he and Weiskopf were level with Miller one behind. Then Nicklaus delivered the Championship-winning blow by holing a monster 40-foot putt for a birdie. The putt broke two ways before going down, much to the delight of the vast gallery.

At the 18th Nicklaus was on in two and ten feet away for a birdie which would have sealed victory. His putt slipped past but he tapped in for par. He was home in 276, the third lowest score in Masters' history, and he waited anxiously by the scorer's tent as Miller and Weiskopf came up the final fairway.

They were level, both one behind Nicklaus, and needing a birdie for a play-off. Miller's 9-iron second shot was 20 feet away from the pin but Weiskopf's second landed within eight feet. Miller missed his birdie putt and his chance of his first Masters was gone. And then to his horror Weiskopf watched as his putt, which was right on line, stopped short. His chance had also gone and Nicklaus became champion for the fifth time.

Nicklaus had won his first Masters in 1963 when he beat Tony Lema by one stroke. His second win in 1965 was by a massive nine strokes from Player and Palmer and when he won it back-to-back in 1966 it was after a three-way play-off. His fourth win, in 1972, was somewhat easier but his record-breaking fifth title was, by far, the hardest of the lot. Miller and Weiskopf pressurized Nicklaus to the end and the Golden Bear's anxious wait as the two of them putted out at the 18th must have been the longest of his life — apart from his *sixth* win 11 years later.

1975 MASTERS STATISTICS

SECOND ROUND LEADERS
135 **Jack Nicklaus** 68-67
140 Billy Casper 70-70
140 Arnold Palmer 69-71
140 Tom Watson 70-70
141 Tom Weiskopf 69-72

THIRD ROUND LEADERS
207 Tom Weiskopf 69-72-66
208 **Jack Nicklaus** 68-67-73
211 Johnny Miller 75-71-65
212 Tom Watson 70-70-72

FINAL SCORES
276 **Jack Nicklaus** 68-67-73-68
277 Johnny Miller 75-71-65-66
277 Tom Weiskopf 69-72-66-70
282 Hale Irwin 73-74-71-64
282 Bobby Nichols 67-74-72-69

NICKLAUS' FOUR OTHER MASTERS' WINS
1963 (**Nicklaus**) 286
Tony Lema 287
1965 (**Nicklaus**) 271
Arnold Palmer 280
Gary Player 280
1966 (**Nicklaus**) 288
Tommy Jacobs 288
Gay Brewer 288
(Nicklaus won play-off 70-72-78)
1972 (**Nicklaus**) 286
Tom Weiskopf 289
Bobby Mitchell 289
Bruce Crampton 289
(Nicklaus added a sixth Masters title in 1986)

Above: Johnny Miller's third round 65 was just one off the Masters' record, but his round included a new record of six consecutive birdies.
Left: Nicklaus, in action during the US Open in 1986, the year of his remarkable sixth Masters title.

RECORDS GALORE AT TURNBERRY

Turnberry is one of the finest golf courses in Scotland yet it was a long time being added to the British Open rota. Situated south of Ayr on Scotland's west coast, the course offers a beautifully scenic background as you look out across the sea to Ailsa Craig, the Island of Arran and the Mull of Kintyre. Its setting is unparalleled among British courses and its entrancing beauty was there for all to see in 1977 when it became the first new course to stage the British Open since Birkdale in 1954.

Turnberry has, however, not always been a course of such beauty. In fact it has lived a troubled life and, had it not been for the devotion of many golf lovers, it could well have closed after the Second World War.

Golf was first played at Turnberry at the turn of the century by the Marquis of Ailsa and by 1907 it had become a favorite golfing center, thanks largely to the attractive adjoining Turnberry Hotel. But, during the First World War the links were used as an airfield. Although some damage was caused it was nowhere near as extensive as that caused when the course was commandeered again during the Second World War. By 1951 all traces of the war had gone, thanks largely to the skills of designer Mackenzie Ross, and the Ailsa Course was soon to stage the Amateur Championship,

Above: 'Oh to be back at Turnberry' . . . Watson struggling with Wentworth's undergrowth!
Above left: Guess who's just sunk a putt?
Left: The beautiful setting of Turnberry's Ailsa course showing the 9th and 10th holes.

Walker Cup and various international matches. But the one championship that had eluded the famous course was the British Open. The course had been, for many years, too easy, but Ross had made it a worthy championship course and in 1977 the world's leading golfers assembled in the Ayrshire town to put Ross' skills to the test.

Hubert Green, the reigning US champion, came to test the course but the man they all had to beat was the man-of-the-moment, Tom Watson. He had won three tournaments on the US Tour before his arrival in Britain, including a Masters win over Jack Nicklaus in April. Watson had won the last British Open to be held in Scotland, at Carnoustie in 1975, after a play-off. He had proved he had the big-match temperament as well as a love of Scottish golf courses. Indeed his love of Scottish courses was confirmed when he won the Open at Muirfield in 1980 and at Troon in 1982.

The par-70 Ailsa course measured 6875 yards but the narrow fairways were made easier because the rough had not grown as much as would have been liked. But there is no such thing as an easy golf course on the west coast of Scotland. As beautiful as Turnberry may be, the weather can change dramatically in no time and thus alter the whole complexion of the course. But glorious sunshine prevailed on the opening day as Turnberry proudly showed itself off to the golfing world.

The Championship committee produced one of those magic pairings such an occasion can offer by putting Henry Cotton and Arnold Palmer together – what a wealth of experience and talent they offered to the Turnberry crowd. Cotton was aged 70 and it was 50 years since he first played in the Open, at St Andrews. He went round Turnberry's first nine holes in 50 and was heading for a three-figure score but he managed to finish with a 93. The crowd wouldn't have cared if he made a 100 – his presence was enough to rekindle nostalgic moments like his three Championship wins at Sandwich in 1934, Carnoustie in 1937 and Muirfield in 1948.

Hale Irwin and Severiano Ballesteros, who had served notice of his presence at Birkdale in 1976, were among the first back in the clubhouse and set the pattern for a low-scoring competition with 70 and 69 respectively. Jack Nicklaus, Lee Trevino and Tom Watson all returned 68s and Nicklaus continued his love affair with the great Scottish courses with a brilliant round, apart from two errors at the second and eighth holes. Watson played a flawless round to show why he was currently the best in the world.

But the big names were overshadowed on the opening day, as so often happens in major championships, by a little-known player. On this occasion it was John Schroeder, son of the 1949 Wimbledon singles champion Ted Schroeder. One of the last out on the course, Schroeder birdied the last two holes for a superb 66.

As Schroeder drifted away on the second day it was time for the 'big guns' to move up and a succession of Open records started to fall. The first record to go was the British Open record of 65 first set by Henry Cotton in 1934 and subsequently equalled by Eric Brown, Leopoldo Ruiz, Peter Butler, Christy O'Connor and Neil Coles. The old figure was shattered by young Mark Hayes from Stillwater, Oklahoma, who needed just 23 putts in his amazing round of 63 which took an agonizing five hours. His two-round total of 139 put him two off the lead held by new leader Roger Maltbie, whose 66 gave him a 137. In between Maltbie and Hayes were a formidable quartet on 138: Hubert Green, Nicklaus, Trevino and Watson. The Scottish bookmakers must have been quivering! Trevino threw away a chance of the outright lead when he three-putted the final green.

Despite the apparent ease of the course and the low scores being returned, players were finding it difficult to remain consistent and only seven men were under par after two rounds. Tony Jacklin, as popular as ever with the British fans, celebrated his 33rd birthday by staying on level par, and just off the lead. But the most satisfying aspect for the former British and US Open champion was the way he played as he turned in some of his best golf for a long time.

Jack Nicklaus and Tom Watson dominated the third round as they matched each other hole-for-hole and both scored 65s. They shared the overall lead by three strokes and set up a classic confrontation for the final day. The 'King' – Nicklaus versus the 'Heir Apparent' – Watson.

Watson had showed no fear of Nicklaus when he beat him by two strokes to win the Masters earlier in the year and here, at Turnberry, he was out-driving

Opposite page: The unmistakable stance of the eventual winner. Watson at the start of the final round at Turnberry in 1977.
Above left: The two men who made the 1977 Open such a memorable tournament, Watson (left) and Nicklaus.
Left: Watson proudly holds aloft the coveted claret jug for the second time in three years.

the Golden Bear and good driving on the Ailsa Course is all-important.

Nicklaus looked like gaining the advantage over Watson during the third round when he led by two but then lightning and torrential rain halted play for an hour and a half. When they resumed Watson drew level after pulling strokes back at the 14th and 15th and despite the awful conditions, these two golfers still returned scores of five under for the day.

The same could not be said for overnight-leader Maltbie, Hubert Green and Lee Trevino. Trevino and Maltbie lost seven strokes to the leaders, while Green lost nine. Nicklaus and Watson were both seven under par for the tournament but the greatness of their three rounds is highlighted by the fact that only four other golfers were under par of 210.

The expected classic finish *did* materialize as the two Americans provided sizzling golf once more, much to the delight of the massive crowd, estimated to be in the region of 18,000. It was one of the largest crowds seen in Scotland and, although a little unruly at times, they very much appreciated the golf played by Watson and Nicklaus.

A brisk breeze swept across the course for the first time all week, but it was not enough to prevent the two central characters returning two more great rounds.

Nicklaus was first to break away with a birdie at the second. His two at the fourth put him three up but Watson showed no fear of the Bear and attacked immediately with a three at the fifth following a brilliant five-iron into the heart of the green. When he looked like losing another stroke at the sixth Watson played a remarkable recovery shot from the sand to save par and then, at the seventh, he pulled one back before levelling at the eighth. Nicklaus, however, stamped his authority on proceedings once more by winning the last hole of the outward nine. He went two up at the 12th but Watson reduced the arrears to one at the next. They both parred 14 and then came the 15th, where the Championship was effectively won – and lost.

Watson's four-iron shot at the par three went to the left of the green and into the light rough. He was lucky to miss the bunker, but he managed to putt out of the rough and into the hole for a two. Nicklaus made par and they were all square for the first time since the eighth hole. That was a 'killer' blow for Nicklaus and although they both got their fours on the next, Watson went for the kill at the 17th when he got a birdie four to Nicklaus' five. Watson had taken 62 for the first 17 to Nicklaus' 63 and that one stroke was all that separated them as they teed off at the 72nd hole.

Watson's drive was perfect, while Nicklaus hit his tee shot perilously close to some unplayable gorse. He recovered with a brilliant second, and Watson's second was perfect as well. Nicklaus sunk his putt for his birdie but Watson had little trouble doing likewise and he raised his arms to salute the vast gallery around the final green who acknowledged him

as a great champion for the second time, while Nicklaus had to be content with the runners-up position for the sixth time!

Both players beat the old British Open record. Watson's total of 268 beat Arnold Palmer's 276 at Troon in 1962 and Tom Weiskopf's 276, also at Troon, in 1973. Nicklaus beat the old record by seven — yet was still a loser!

Watson also added the record for the lowest two rounds, the lowest aggregate for the first 54 holes and lowest for the last 54. The crowd totalled more than 92,000, which was a British Open record for Scotland and the domination of the tournament by American golfers was never more evident as they filled the first eight places.

At the top of the pile was a man who had matured in such a short space of time. Watson had jumped from 224th to 1st in the US Tour money list in just six years. A popular winner, he was certainly a worthy successor to Nicklaus and he has gone on to capture a total of five British Open titles and that is something even the great man himself has not done (or at least not yet!)

Watson and Nicklaus may have treated the course with little respect but it must not be forgotten that the third man, Hubert Green, was 11 strokes behind Watson. Turnberry had arrived on the British Open scene, and to win the Open you have to beat the course and the best golfers in the world. Tom Watson did just that even though the final round became a two-man match between him and Nicklaus.

The large crowds were testament to the organisers' judgement that the time was right to take the championship to the Ayrshire course. The organization was superb considering the large galleries and that was to be the case when Turnberry was next used for the Open in 1986. On that occasion, Australian Greg Norman won a 'one-horse' race, but a toughening up of the course meant no records fell like they had done in 1977.

Right: Watson's 268 beat the Open record by eight shots, and still remains the championship record.

FINAL SCORES

268 **Tom Watson** (USA)	68-70-65-65
269 Jack Nicklaus (USA)	68-70-65-66
279 Hubert Green (USA)	72-66-74-67
280 Lee Trevino (USA)	68-70-72-70
281 Ben Crenshaw (USA)	71-69-66-75
281 George Burns (USA)	70-70-72-69
282 Arnold Palmer (USA)	73-73-67-69
283 Ray Floyd (USA)	70-73-68-72
284 Tommy Horton (GB)	70-74-65-75
284 Johnny Miller (USA)	69-74-67-74
284 John Schroeder (USA)	66-74-73-71
284 Mark Hayes (USA)	76-63-72-73

TURNBERRY 1977 STATISTICS

Mark Hayes' record-breaking round

Hole	1	2	3	4	5	6	7	8	9	Out	10	11	12	13	14	15	16	17	18	In	Total
Length	355	428	462	167	411	222	528	427	455	3455	452	177	391	411	440	209	409	500	431	3420	6875
Par	4	4	4	3	4	3	5	4	4	35	4	3	4	4	4	3	4	5	4	35	70
Hayes	4	3	3	3	4	3	4	4	4	32	4	2	3	4	4	3	3	3	5	31	63

Nicklaus' and Watson's final round

Hole	1	2	3	4	5	6	7	8	9	Out	10	11	12	13	14	15	16	17	18	In	Total
Length	355	428	462	167	411	222	528	427	455	3455	452	177	391	411	440	209	409	500	431	3420	6875
Par	4	4	4	3	4	3	5	4	4	35	4	3	4	4	4	3	4	5	4	35	70
Nicklaus	4	3	4	2	4	3	5	4	4	33	4	3	4	4	3	4	5	3	33	66
Watson	4	5	4	3	3	3	4	3	5	34	4	3	4	3	4	2	4	4	3	31	65

GARY PLAYER'S THIRD MASTERS

In 1957, a diminutive 22-year-old South African made his first raid on the United States golf circuit. That man, Gary Player, was to become one of the most popular and pleasant overseas players to compete on the US Tour over the next 20 years or more.

Player competed in his first Masters during that season and finished equal 24th. He failed to qualify the following year but did register his first win on American soil when he won the Kentucky Derby Open, and he also finished second to Tommy Bolt in the Open at Southern Hills, Tulsa. In 1961, however, he was leading money winner on the Tour and was Masters Champion for the first time, beating Arnold Palmer and Charlie Coe by one stroke.

He became a regular on the Tour and was the first overseas player seriously to challenge the best Americans on their own territory and he consistently figured high among the money winners. In 1974 he won his second Masters title when he was two ahead of Dave Stockton and Tom Weiskopf, but when he arrived at Augusta in 1978 there were few that had Player among the front runners for the title. After three rounds of the Georgia course their judgement seemed to be correct, but then came an explosive final day, the like of which has rarely been seen in championship golf.

Player was over 42 years of age but, despite his age, the keep-fit fanatic from Johannesburg arrived at Augusta with a 31-inch waistline and weighed in at 150 pounds, just as he had done when he first appeared in the Masters 21 years earlier.

The presence of the friendly South African is always a welcome sight on any golf course the world over but his presence was overshadowed on this occasion by that of Jack Nicklaus who emerged as the clear favorite to win the 42nd Masters, and his sixth title.

Nicklaus dragged himself away from his multi-million-dollar business enterprise to compete and was, despite his limited appearances, still top money winner going into the Masters having won two and finished second in two more of the five events he had contested leading up to the big one. Fellow professional Chi Chi Rodriguez, making obvious reference to Jack's limited appearances, described Nicklaus as: 'A spare-time legend.'

The legend, as he can rightly be called, was enjoying his success with a 9½-degree loft driver as opposed to his usual 12-degree club. He had tried a 9½-degree club some years earlier but lost accuracy at

Top: 'That fits lovely'; Player after his first Masters win in 1961. Arnold Palmer makes the presentation.
Above: Nicklaus and Player, two men who have provided the Augusta National with some great moments over the years.
Above right: Fellow South African Bobby Locke (left) with Player (center) after Player's first professional win in 1956. Locke won the British Open four times in the 1950s.

54

the expense of distance. Now he got them both right and he was out-driving most of his rivals.

Hubert Green and defending champion Tom Watson were considered the real serious challengers to the Golden Bear, while the youngster Severiano Ballesteros, who had become the youngest US Tour winner since Ray Floyd in 1963 when he won the Greensboro Open the week before the Masters, was regarded as a threat. But there was little talk of Gary Player as the next winner of the coveted green jacket.

Player was one of 10 overseas invitees in the field of 78 who teed off on the first day. The severe winter had affected the usually beautiful blooms that are Augusta's trade mark and the course appeared to be easier than usual but then Augusta has that ability to lull the unsuspecting golfer into a false sense of security. The course must be treated with respect.

The first day belonged to 38-year-old John Schlee, the golf director of the Rancho Viejo Country Club in Texas, who shot a four-under-par 68 to lead Joe Inman by one. Inman was the last man out on the course and was also four under until he bogeyed the 17th and finished with 69.

Schlee, 6 feet 3 inches tall and with greying-brown hair, was the 1966 Rookie of the Year and runner-up to Johnny Miller in the 1973 Open at Oakmont. He had quit the US Tour in 1977 because of injuries and took up the job in Texas. Four consecutive birdies at 'Amen Corner', the 12th, 13th, 14th and 15th, set him up for his tournament-leading round. A perfectionist at taking the right club for the right shot Schlee was so concerned at taking the wrong club at the par-3 12th during the 1977 Masters that he borrowed the gallery rope to measure the distance for himself, believing the card to be wrong!

Although the 1978 Masters started with the temperature well into the eighties, a strong breeze prevailed and this breeze, and the tough pin placements, particularly for a first day, made conditions deceptively difficult and some high scoring resulted.

Nicklaus returned a 37 and 35 for level par but had he not missed four short putts, all from under five feet, he would have been up with Schlee. Player had two halves of 36, also for his par. Lee Trevino, who rarely plays well in the Masters, was two under on 70 and was as confident as ever about winning his first

GARY PLAYER'S THIRD MASTERS

title. Back surgery toward the end of 1976 had relieved an injury that had troubled him since the day he was struck by lightning at the Butler National, Illinois, in 1975. Back to peak fitness, and form, Trevino had gained 20 to 30 yards on his drives and was playing as well as ever. One of his most spectacular drives, at the par-five second, was estimated at being around 380 yards.

Trevino, sensing this could be his year, cut down the clowning and it certainly helped as he became one of the joint leaders on day two. He added a 69 to his first-round 70 to share the lead on 139 with Rod Funseth. A year before, Funseth had shot a second-round 66 to share the lead with Tom Watson before Watson went on to win the Masters. Maybe that was an omen for Trevino?

Funseth, who celebrated his 45th birthday on the Monday before the start of the Masters, had been on the Tour 18 years and, by his own admission, does not expect to win anything. A great character who thoroughly enjoys his golf, he does, however, lack confidence. He is once reported as asking, when involved in a play-off for the Greensboro Open: 'How much is the second prize?' He also says he would like to retire a millionaire but added: 'I can't figure out a way to make a million.'

Opposite page: Player, a master at playing out of sand.
Left: Gary Player, seen here after his success in the 1968 British Open at Carnoustie, has won majors in three decades.
Below: The club house at the Augusta National course, where Gary Player is always made welcome.

What a pair of characters to have at the top of the leader board, but Trevino was quite content to let Funseth do the clowning while he got down to the serious business of trying to win his first Masters.

The weather, once again, was very hot for the time of the year but the greens were slow because of the abundance of grass, but they suited Hale Irwin and Gene Littler who shot 67 and 68 respectively to move one stroke behind the two leaders. The first-day leader John Schlee moved out to 143 after a 75, and Nicklaus was six behind the leaders, while Player was tied in 16th place on 144.

Tommy Nakajima has a knack of getting himself into the news at the majors but often for the wrong reasons. He took a 13 at the par-five 13th. Later that year he was to take a nine at St Andrews' Road Hole after reaching the green in two.

Conditions on day three were ideal for low scoring as the warm weather was not accompanied by the winds that had been swirling around the Augusta course. The third round normally does the 'sorting out' and the two big overnight questions were: would Trevino consolidate his lead and, would Nicklaus come through with one of his great rounds? The answers to both questions were – no.

While Nicklaus carded a 69, he was again let down by his short putting and his three-round total of 214 was eight behind the new leader Hubert Green. Gary Player was seven behind Green after a 69, but Lee Trevino bid farewell to his chance when he had a triple bogey seven at the easy 5th.

The new hero was Hubert Green, the man with hardly any backswing and generally one of the most unorthodox swings in golf. But, despite his style, he made few mistakes for a sizzling 65, just one off the Masters record, to go into a three-stroke lead. What few mistakes he did make were compensated by great recovery shots as he emerged the favorite to add the Masters to the Heritage Classic he had won a couple of weeks earlier.

Above: The characteristic swing and familiar all-black attire, Player in action at Augusta.
Above left: Player with fellow South African Harold Henning and Jack Nicklaus, one of their opponents during the 1971 World Cup.

Green had to contend with Tom Watson who was coming into the sort of form that won him the title twelve months earlier. After a bad opening 73 the defending champion shot two consecutive 68s to share second place on 209 with Rod Funseth, who was still there after a 70. But Watson, who partnered Green during the third round, was impressed with the man from Alabama's round and, when asked how he was going to beat Green, Watson said: 'Put a contract out on him!'

But as Green, Watson and the thousands of Augusta customers know only too well, three strokes can easily disappear in one hole on this course. But what those fans did not know when the final day started was that they were to witness one of the tightest finishes in the long history of the great tournament.

Gary Player started the final round seven behind Green but openly said he felt confident. But who could honestly believe, despite the South African's self-confidence, that he could win his third title. But he went out and strung together seven birdies in the last 10 holes to put him in the clubhouse with a record-equalling 64.

Player's partner on his final round was the young Spaniard Ballesteros, who was celebrating his 21st birthday. They were six groups ahead of the leaders and Player started his round with a birdie four at the second, despite a three wood into the sand. But the South African is the best sand player in the world as a result of hours and hours of practice chipping out of bunkers as a youngster, and he recovered brilliantly for his birdie.

Player found time for one moment of light relief during his round of great concentration, when a chip at the 11th rolled around the hole and stayed out. Uncharacteristically the South African lay on his back and kicked his legs in the air. When he realized what he had done, he turned to his gallery and quickly apologized!

Hubert Green played consistent golf, never fluctuating more than one above or below par for the day, but it was not good enough as his three-stroke lead soon evaporated and he was hauled back to join Watson and Funseth. All three were joined by the advancing Player and, at one stage, the leader board showed a four-way tie. The pre-tournament favorite Jack Nicklaus showed what he could do to the Augusta course as he shot a final round 67, but it was too late, and the 1978 Masters was left to four men.

Player was safely in the clubhouse, watching and waiting to see if his one-stroke lead over the others would be enough. The tournament was decided on the 18th green as all three, in turn, had a chance to level Player and force a play-off. Green, Watson and Funseth each needed a birdie at the last to stay alive and all three had possible birdie putts.

Green had the easiest of the three as he needed a 30-inch putt to level with Player. He addressed the ball but backed away when a broadcaster disturbed him. When he lined it up a second time, he missed but

did not blame the commentator, he blamed himself. It was a bad putt, and he knew it. Watson's putt was tougher at 12 feet. He missed as well. And Funseth had a near impossible task from 24 feet, but he came close with the ball stopping just inches from the hole. Funseth had been in with a chance going into the final nine holes of his last four majors but had come away empty-handed. He was not disappointed, however, because he knew he had played well, and he also knew he did not throw the Masters away; Gary Player had to win it.

Player was relieved it did not go to a play-off as it would have been sudden-death and he revealed afterwards that he had lost 17 such play-offs. This was Player's 19th win on the US Tour, his 112th worldwide and his third Masters. Now at the age of 42 years 5 months 9 days, and 17 years after his first title, Gary Player had become the oldest winner of the Masters.

ROUND ONE
68	John Schlee
69	Joe Inman
70	Lee Trevino
70	Bill Kratzert
(72	**Gary Player**)

ROUND TWO
139	Rod Funseth 73-66
139	Lee Trevino 70-69
140	Hale Irwin 73-67
140	Gene Littler 72-68
(144	**Gary Player** 72-72)

ROUND THREE
206	Hubert Green 72-69-65
209	Tom Watson 73-68-68
209	Rod Funseth 73-66-70
210	Gene Littler 72-68-70
(213	**Gary Player** 72-72-69)

FINAL SCORE
277	**Gary Player** 72-72-69-64
278	Rod Funseth 73-66-70-69
278	Hubert Green 72-69-65-72
278	Tom Watson 73-68-68-69

Above left: A bespectacled Arnold Palmer with Player during practice for the Masters.
Left: Green jacket number three for the likeable South African. The presentation is traditionally made by the winner of the previous year's tournament, in this case Tom Watson.
Right: The style that has made Gary Player one of the best short-game golfers in the world.

THE EUROPEAN BREAKTHROUGH

American golf fans were given the first indication of the greatness of Severiano Ballesteros when he came from 10 strokes behind after two rounds to win the 1978 Greater Greensboro Open. The same year he competed in his first Masters and Jack Nicklaus commented that before he was through, the young, handsome, Spaniard would win many titles at Augusta. Two years later, Nicklaus's forecast came true as Ballesteros lifted his first Masters title.

Born in Santander, northern Spain, Ballesteros lived on his father's farm which adjoined the local golf course and his first taste of the sport was caddying for his eldest brother Manuel. It was not long before Sevvy was swinging a club in earnest and he soon became a better player than his brother.

A regular on the European Tour since 1974, when his £2915 prize money put him 118th on the money list, his first big win was the Dutch Open two years later. Despite efforts to get him to join the US Tour after his Greensboro win, Ballesteros remained loyal to the European circuit and established himself as the number one player in Europe. He still regularly visited America, and his style of play was always welcomed. He first came to international prominence when, as a relative unknown, he pushed Johnny Miller all the way in the 1976 British Open at Birkdale.

He came to Georgia in 1980 for the 44th Masters, not only as the reigning British Open champion, the best player, and biggest hitter, in Europe, but as one of the best in the world and he posed a definite threat to the American monopoly of the Masters title. While South African Gary Player had won the title three times, no European had worn the famous green jacket. Few had even come close to winning the title. Perhaps the best chance was by Britain's Peter Oosterhuis in 1973 when he threw away a three-stroke lead going into the final round to finish equal third behind Tommy Aaron and Jesse Snead.

But now there was a real chance that golf's new superstar from across the Atlantic could lift one of the sport's most cherished prizes, but Nicklaus was still around and he can never be discounted on such an occasion and he, Tom Watson and Lee Trevino all missed the previous week's Greensboro Open to practice for the Masters. There were also the perils the Augusta course always has to offer and Ballesteros was noted for his wayward shots followed by great recoveries, like the previous year's British Open at Royal Lytham when he chipped up for a birdie from

Above: Ballesteros after winning his first US Tour event, the 1978 Greater Greensboro Open.
Above right: The Spaniard flirting with danger, and overcoming it in a typical display of power golf.
Below right: The salute that marks another victory for Ballesteros.

the parking lot. But Augusta will not permit too many wayward shots.

Heavy rain during the practice days had made the greens slower than usual, and a brisk wind on the first day ensured that scores were high, but Ballesteros, Australian David Graham and American Jeff Mitchell opened with 66s to share the lead. Only 18 players broke par, making the leading three's six under even more impressive.

The wind got more devastating as the day went on, swirling in and out of the trees and it certainly fooled Jack Nicklaus who slumped to a 74, including a double bogey at the 12th after going into the infamous Rae's Creek. Ed Sneed, who bogeyed the last three holes in 1979 to go into a three-way play-off with Fuzzy Zoeller and Tom Watson before losing to Zoeller, carried on where he left off with bogeys at 17 and 18 for a first round total of 79. But Nicklaus and Sneed had little to worry about compared to Tom Weiskopf who equalled the Masters record for the

THE EUROPEAN BREAKTHROUGH

Above: Ballesteros after his first major victory, in the 1979 British Open.

Left: Sheer power got this ball out of the trap from a difficult lie, Ballesteros on his way to victory at Royal Lytham in the 1979 British Open. Ben Crenshaw shared second place with Jack Nicklaus whose record in the British Open includes three victories.

most strokes taken at one hole – 13. Weiskopf hit five balls into Rae's Creek at the 12th for his 13 and then, at the next hole, he dumped one in another stretch of the same creek for a bogey six!

But the day belonged to Ballesteros, who was celebrating his 23rd birthday. Renowned as the longest hitter in Europe, his big hitting often resulted in a lack of accuracy as his 1979 British Open record of hitting only two fairways on the last day's play indicated. But now he had cut down on his distance to get the accuracy right, which is vital at Augusta, and this change resulted in him *missing* just one fairway. He had four birdies and a bogey in the first nine for a 33, then three birdies in the back nine for another 33.

Above: Sevvy on his way to his first Masters title.
Right: Ballesteros' success at Augusta paved the way for other European golfers to enjoy success in the United States.

One of Ballesteros' co-leaders, David Graham, adapted to the windy conditions because many of the courses in his home country often had swirling winds around them, and the reigning PGA Champion used them to full advantage for his 66. Graham, a regular on the US Tour and living in Florida, still retained his Australian citizenship. Also sharing the lead was 26-year-old Jeff Mitchell from Rockford, Illinois. A Tour member since 1976 he was fulfilling a life-long dream by playing in the Masters, and for a man still to register his first Tour win, to be joint leader must have been beyond the wildest of his dreams.

The first noticeable piece of action from the second day was the improvement of Tom Weiskopf . . . he put only two balls into Rae's Creek at the 12th for a seven for an improved round of 79 – giving a total of 20 over par!

Joint leaders Mitchell and Graham shot 75 and 73 and Ballesteros took full advantage of their slip to hit a 69 and build up a four-stroke lead over Graham and Rex Caldwell, who had joined the Australian in second place after a fine 66. But Ballesteros had to work hard for his 69 after he returned to his wayward driving accompanied by great recovery shots.

The Spaniard showed a total disregard for obstacles as he sprayed his tee shots all over the course. At the 17th his drive landed on the seventh green and, after picking off, he hit a seven iron, blind, to within 15-feet of the pin for a birdie putt. He had six birdies in his round and in making four of them his drive failed to hit the fairway at all! A typical example of his round was at the par-five second where he hooked his tee shot, it hit a tree and bounced on to the fairway. He took a one iron which flew to the right of the green but recovered with a wedge to within 10 feet before making his birdie. The style of the Spaniard, who certainly makes play more interesting for the spectator, was likened to the young Arnold Palmer, and even Arnie would not disagree with that comparison.

The half-way cut was made at 146 and Palmer, Nicklaus, Trevino, and Johnny Miller all made it to day three, but with little to spare. Despite their reputations, there seemed little anybody could do to halt the Spaniard's charge.

Ballesteros' job was made easier by not having any big names chasing him and he virtually won the 1980 Masters on day three when he stretched his lead to seven shots over 26-year-old Texan Ed Fiori, playing his first Masters, thanks to a 68 which put him 13 under, and in contention for an all-time tournament record.

He played his third round as if it was a Pro-Am event: relaxed and at a leisurely pace. It certainly helped him get over his erratic driving on the second round as he only missed one fairway all day. His round contained, surprisingly, four bogeys, including one at the first hole of the day. But, at the four par-fives he had one eagle and three birdies and, for the third day in succession, he had a 33 for the back nine, including three consecutive birdies.

It was Tom Watson's turn to have a disaster at the 12th as he put two balls into Rae's Creek, but the seventh and eighth holes of Fiori must rank as some sort of record as he had a double bogey at seven, followed by an eagle at eight.

While Ballesteros' presence and style of play were making for attractive watching, the final round pairing of Jack Nicklaus and Arnold Palmer was one of sheer nostalgia and, while neither was in with a chance, they still attracted a large percentage of the huge gallery. Palmer won their private battle by leaping ahead of Nicklaus with a 69 for 288, while Jack had a 73 for 291. But, while they were enjoying their private 18-hole battle, Ballesteros was, first of all seeming invincible, and then looking shaky, as he fought his way through the last 18 holes of the 1980 Masters.

He increased his lead to 10 strokes at one stage, but later only led by two. What happened to the brilliant Spaniard?

He birdied three of the first six holes, thanks again to the 'Harry Houdini' impersonation, and the Masters record was certainly on the cards. But then he three putted to bogey the 10th, hit the creek for a

double bogey at 12, and found the creek again for another bogey at 13. It was beginning to look as though the sub-par scores of Hubert Green, Jack Newton (Ballesteros' playing partner), and Gibby Gilbert were going to provide an unexpected threat to Europe's top player. After 13 holes the Spaniard was 12 under, while Gilbert was just two behind on 10 under, with Newton one stroke behind him. Any more bogeys and it would be complete disaster for Ballesteros, but he eased off the self-inflicted pressure with a birdie at the 15th and then pars all the way home and that run, together with Gilbert's bogey at 18, assured Sevvy of his first Masters title, although it was not the runaway victory that was expected. But that is what makes the appeal of the young man so magnetic, you never know what he will do next, or how he will do it.

Gilbert and Newton shared second place on 279 and the 39-year-old Gilbert from Chattanooga came his nearest ever to winning a major. For Newton it was another 'near-miss' to add to his 1975 British Open catastrophe. But the 44th Masters had been dominated by one man – Severiano Ballesteros, who became, at 23 years 4 days, the youngest winner of the title, nearly three months younger than Nicklaus when he won in 1963. More important, he became the first European winner of the title and that set the pattern for the 1980s when he went on to win it a second time, and West Germany's Bernhard Langer also won the title, to end the US domination.

Left: David Graham (top) and Gibby Gilbert (bottom) both made up ground on Ballesteros in the final round of the 1980 Masters but could not catch him.
Top: The revival of European golf was completed in 1985 when they won the Ryder Cup. Ballesteros (second left) is seen with fellow Spaniards (from left) Pinero, Canizares and Rivero.
Above: Ballesteros drives off during the 1984 British Open at St Andrews.

ROUND ONE

66	**Severiano Ballesteros**
66	Jeff Mitchell
66	David Graham
68	Jack Newton
68	Hubert Green

ROUND TWO

135	**Severiano Ballesteros**	66-69
139	Rex Caldwell	73-66
139	David Graham	66-73
140	Jerry Pate	72-68
140	Jim Simons	70-70
140	Ed Sneed	70-70
140	Doug Tewell	71-69
140	Tom Kite	69-71

ROUND THREE

203	**Severiano Ballesteros**	66-69-68
210	Ed Fiori	71-70-69
211	Jack Newton	68-74-69
211	Andy North	70-72-69
211	David Graham	66-73-72
211	Jesse Sneed	73-69-69

FINAL SCORE

275	**Severiano Ballesteros**	66-69-68-72
279	Jack Newton	68-74-69-68
279	Gibby Gilbert	70-74-68-67
280	Hubert Green	68-74-71-67
281	David Graham	66-73-72-70

THE 1985 RYDER CUP

In October 1983 Tony Jacklin's band of confident golfers arrived at the PGA National Club in Florida for the 25th playing of the Ryder Cup and only a Tom Watson victory over Bernard Gallacher prevented the unthinkable from happening – defeat on home soil for the Americans for the first time ever. As it was, they hung on for a narrow 14½-13½ victory; but the signs at Palm Beach Gardens that October day indicated it was going to be a tough battle on British soil two years later if the Americans were going to avoid their first Ryder Cup defeat since 1957 when Great Britain & Northern Ireland won by three points.

Since their last win the constitution and name of the Great Britain team had been changed to that of 'Europe' in 1979, when continental players were drafted into the team in an effort to wrest the trophy from the Americans. It failed in 1979 and 1981, but came close in 1983 as former British and US Open winner Tony Jacklin blended together a quality team. After his near success at Florida, he had two years planning before the next assault, at his own PGA's headquarters at the Belfry, in September 1985.

American fans could hardly have failed to notice how European golfers were beginning to dominate the world circuit. Seve Ballesteros had won his second Masters title in 1983 and Bernhard Langer and Sandy Lyle went into this latest Ryder Cup match as holders of the Masters and British Open titles. The likes of Langer and Ballesteros had proved they had the ability to win on American courses and they were obviously going to be hard to beat when they were playing on British soil.

Below: The complete 1985 US Ryder Cup team.
Opposite: The picturesque setting of the 10th green at the Belfry, venue of the 1985 Ryder Cup.

70

The Belfry provides one of the most beautiful settings in English golf on a course that was only officially opened in 1977. Its par-72 7176 yards has many lakes as a prominent feature and the setting was ideal for its first Ryder Cup match.

Most of the Americans flew into Birmingham International Airport by Concorde, while the remainder arrived on a Fokker Friendship from Switzerland where they had been competing in the Ebel Swiss Masters, which Craig Stadler won ahead of several of his Ryder Cup opponents – and team mates. On paper the teams were as close as they had been for many years. While the Americans did not have big names like Tom Watson, Ben Crenshaw and Jack Nicklaus in their line-up, it was a testament to the strength-in-depth of American golf that men like Peter Jacobsen, Mark O'Meara, Hal Sutton and Andy North, all making their Ryder Cup débuts, could merit selection to take their places.

US Captain Lee Trevino left out reigning US Open and PGA title holders, Andy North and Hubert Green, for the opening foursomes and Tony Jacklin made a late change to the European team bringing in Manuel Pinero to play with Ballesteros, instead of José Rivero. But despite the air of confidence among Jacklin's team they trailed 3-1 at the end of the first morning foursomes and it looked like an all too familiar Ryder Cup pattern was to begin unfolding for the European team.

The first morning did, however, start on a note of optimism for the European team as Severiano Ballesteros gave the home fans plenty to cheer about at 8.20 am when he holed a 10-foot putt for a birdie at the first hole. Although he and Pinero went on to beat Curtis Strange and Mark O'Meara 2 & 1 that was the only high point for their team in an otherwise dismal morning.

The anticipated star pairing of Langer and Nick Faldo was not good enough for Calvin Peete and Tom Kite who won 3 & 2 with Peete, the second black Ryder Cup player after Lee Elder, showing no signs of the shoulder injury that had restricted his playing in the six weeks prior to the match. Tom Kite enjoys the Ryder Cup and he will be remembered for his great play the last time the Cup was contested on English soil, at Walton Heath in 1981, when he had a memorable match with Sandy Lyle at the end of which Lyle was eight under par and lost because Kite was *10* under.

Ray Floyd, the oldest man in the competition, and his partner Lanny Wadkins, beat British Open champion Lyle and Ken Brown 4 & 3. The performance of both the European golfers left a lot to be desired and skipper Jacklin promptly removed them from the list of players selected to play in the afternoon session.

Left: Despite a win in the foursomes with Calvin Peete, and a half with Ballesteros in the singles, Tom Kite could not prevent a European victory.

Wadkins, like Kite, loves Ryder Cup matches and who will ever forget the sight of US captain Jack Nicklaus kissing a divot made by Wadkins as he played a magnificent pitch to within 12 inches of the flag at the 18th in 1983?

Craig Stadler and Hal Sutton completed the morning session with a 3 & 2 win over Howard Clark and Sam Torrance and the Americans went into lunch with a two-point lead. Normally such a lead would demoralize the European contingent, but not this team.

Jacklin introduced youngsters Paul Way and Ian Woosnam into the act for the afternoon fourballs and they responded with a magnificent one-hole win over Hubert Green and Fuzzy Zoeller, holders of four majors between them. Way and Woosnam, however, had to fight off a challenge from the two experienced Americans before snatching their victory. Way birdied the 10th to put his team three up but the American pair threw everything at the two Britons, produc-

ing five birdies in seven holes to draw level going into the 18th. Such pressure would have been sufficient to cause many British players to wither but not these two. Way was the hero of the hour with a 220-yard second shot that landed within 10 feet of the pin. He made his birdie putt and the European side were back in the match.

Ballesteros and Pinero commanded their second match right from the start and Peter Jacobsen and Andy North could not counteract it. And when Ballesteros drove the 275-yard par-four 10th, with a three wood, to within 20 feet of the pin, the large section of the 25,000 crowd following this match sensed another home victory was on the cards. Ballesteros missed his eagle putt, but another birdie at the next virtually assured the Spaniards of victory, which came at the 17th, and suddenly the match was all square.

In the other two matches still out on the course Langer and Jose-Maria Canizares led Stadler and Sut-

ton by one with seven to play and Torrance and Clark were level with Ray Floyd and Lanny Wadkins with four to play. The match was evenly poised and the Europeans looked as though they were heading for a one-point lead at the end of the first day, just as they had done at Florida two years earlier. But, suddenly, it all changed.

Stadler and Sutton had three birdies in the last six holes compared with Langer and Canizares' two, and the American pair managed to halve the match. At the last hole Langer's 18-foot putt finished just three inches short, thus depriving the home team of their third win of the afternoon. So, with one match still out on the course, the scores were level but more cruel luck was in store for the Europeans.

Below: Bernhard Langer looking more than a little happy after sinking a long putt.
Right: After losing his opening day's foursomes with Nick Faldo, West Germany's Bernhard Langer did not lose another match in the 1985 Ryder Cup.

Above: Misses like this one of Stadler's cost the United States team dearly.
Right: Fuzzy Zoeller had a miserable third Ryder Cup. He lost all three of his matches.

Having matched each other hole-for-hole over the back nine, Floyd and Wadkins gained a one-hole advantage over Torrance and Clark at the 16th. At the final hole Torrance had a terrible drive but then salvaged the situation with a second to within four feet. Wadkins, however, after a good drive, messed up his second and was 25-feet away. But, as often happens, Torrance missed his easy putt, Wadkins sank his, and the United States ended the first day 4½-3½ to the good.

Considering the score at the end of the morning session, Tony Jacklin must have been pleased with the overnight score and, considering the fire in the bellies of the European players, Lee Trevino must have been *delighted* at his first-day lead.

Jacklin brought Sandy Lyle back into the action for the fourballs on the second morning. He played him alongside Langer, but it was the tested pairing of Torrance and Clark that opened the day with a win for the Europeans, beating Kite and North 2 & 1. The youngsters, Way and Woosnam, continued their great run of success by chalking up their second win over Zoeller and Green. This time they played with far more confidence and ran out easy 4 & 3 winners after being five up after eight holes. Their win put the home team in the lead but, when they were expected to build on that through the experience of Ballesteros and Pinero, the two Spaniards lost to O'Meara and Wadkins 3 & 2 and once more the two teams were all

square. But the turning point of the morning's play, and possibly of the whole match, came in the final pairing of the second day's fourballs.

The new pairing of Lyle and Langer was two down to Stadler and Strange with two to play, and then Lyle sank a monster putt at the 17th to pull one back. At the 18th Stadler had a two-footer to halve the hole and win the match but he missed and, at the half-way stage, the match remained evenly poised at six points apiece.

The easy miss by Stadler prompted Tony Jacklin to recall how such an incident can put you off the rest of your game. 'You never like to win holes like that,' he said, and added: 'I remember a Mexican guy chipping in during the 1972 Open at Muirfield.' He was, of course, referring to his opposing captain who 'stole' the title from him by holing two chips and a bunker shot, and recalled that he never recovered from Trevino's piece of good fortune. The same happened to Stadler. He was put off his game and he and Hal Sutton lost their afternoon foursomes to Ballesteros and Pinero 5 & 4.

Jacklin introduced a fourth Spaniard for the four-somes on the second afternoon when he brought in José Rivero to play alongside José-Maria Canizares, and what a duo they turned out to be as Tom Kite and Calvin Peete could not respond to their blistering play and found themselves four down at the end of the outward nine holes. Defeat came for the American pair on the 13th as the two Europeans registered a magnificent 7 & 5 victory.

After the first two foursomes the Europeans had pulled away to lead 8-6 and that missed putt of Stadler's was beginning to have a devastating effect and,

despite all his powers of verbal persuasion, Trevino seemed unable to get the message 'to forget it' over to his team.

Curtis Strange and Peter Jacobsen did their best to get the Americans back into the match by eventually inflicting defeat upon the seemingly invincible pairing of Way and Woosnam. Despite their defeat, nobody could deny their vast contribution to the European lead. Bernhard Langer and Ken Brown, however, kept the home fans happy by winding up the second day's proceedings with a fine 3 & 2 win over Floyd and Wadkins. It meant that for the first

Manuel Pinero was the first to increase the score with a 3 & 1 win over Lanny Wadkins, thanks to three birdies in the first six holes of the inward nine which saw off the Texan. Craig Stadler cut the lead back to two points after he beat Welshman Ian Woosnam who had certainly enjoyed a successful second Ryder Cup outing. But then Paul Way, the 22-year-old from Middlesex, and star of the European team, showed a coolness that defied his years in beating Ray Floyd who had been winning on the professional tour since 1963, 22 years before.

The English player was four up at the eighth but Floyd's experience saw him chip away at that lead and he was only one down going into the 18th, but the youngster held on and Floyd conceded the last. That was the first time either player had given anything since Way refused to give Floyd an easy putt at the second in an incident that added an air of tension to their match. Way's win restored the three-point advantage and the pressure was heavily on the defending team.

Ballesteros forced a half from nowhere against Tom Kite thanks to three birdies in the last five holes as a result of successful putts from 45 feet at the 14th, 15 feet at the 15th and 12 feet at the 17th. Sandy Lyle, at last, played his best golf and ended Peter Jacobsen's hopes with a 45-foot putt for a birdie three at the 16th. Europe led by four with just seven pairings out on the course, but most of them were close and it could still have gone either way.

Langer's match with Sutton was one of those that was not close and he won 5 & 4 at the 14th to increase the lead to five with just six left to come in. Howard Clark, Sam Torrance and José Rivero all had chances to make the match-winning putt for Tony Jacklin's team and it was fitting that the much-loved Scot, Torrance, should have the honor of clinching the Cup at 4 o'clock, on that memorable Sunday afternoon.

Torrance was playing in his third Ryder Cup and he and Andy North were level as they teed off at the 18th. The Scot hit the best drive of his life, while North put his drive into the lake. Torrance knew he had won the Cup for Europe. As he walked up the fairway he could not hold back his emotions as he shed tears of joy but he was not alone in shedding those tears. Many of the large gallery joined him, including his father Bob who was somewhere among the vast army of followers. The noise from the crowd was deafening as Torrance sank his final putt, ironically to take the lead over North for the first time in their match. The other players out on the course knew what had happened. The rest was academic as Howard Clark and Canizares both added more victories to the European score but, they, and all the European players just wanted to get their hands on the trophy – and the champagne.

Left: After a poor start Sandy Lyle showed how he could really play.
Right: The Cup-winner, Scotland's Sam Torrance, celebrates sinking his final putt in the decisive singles match.

time since 1949 a Great Britain (or European) side was going into the final day's singles with a two-point lead. On that occasion the Americans turned the score around to win by two points, but these latest challengers were playing with great confidence and their American counterparts had lost a lot of theirs. Victory was certainly there for the taking by Tony Jacklin and his men.

Thirty thousand partisan fans filled the Sutton Coldfield course for the final day's play in blustery conditions. While they did not witness the best golf in the world, they did see a great display of self control and determination from their heroes.

SCORES: DAY ONE

Europe		United States	
Foursomes			
S. Ballesteros & M. Pinero	BEAT	C. Strange & M. O'Meara	2 & 1
B. Langer & N. Faldo	LOST TO	C. Peete & T. Kite	3 & 2
A. Lyle & K. Brown	LOST TO	L. Wadkins & R. Floyd	4 & 3
H. Clark & S. Torrance	LOST TO	C. Stadler & H. Sutton	3 & 2
Fourballs			
P. Way & I. Woosnam	BEAT	F. Zoeller & H. Green	1 hole
S. Ballesteros & M. Pinero	BEAT	A. North & P. Jacobsen	2 & 1
B. Langer & J-M. Canizares	HALVED	C. Stadler & H. Sutton	
S. Torrance & H. Clark	LOST TO	R. Floyd & L. Wadkins	1 hole

Score: Europe 3½ United States 4½

SCORES: DAY TWO

Europe		United States	
Fourballs			
S. Torrance & H. Clark	BEAT	T. Kite & A. North	2 & 1
P. Way & I. Woosnam	BEAT	H. Green & F. Zoeller	4 & 3
S. Ballesteros & M. Pinero	LOST TO	M. O'Meara & L. Wadkins	3 & 2
B. Langer & A. Lyle	HALVED	C. Stadler & C. Strange	
Foursomes			
J-M. Canizares & J. Rivero	BEAT	T. Kite & C. Peete	7 & 5
S. Ballesteros & M. Pinero	BEAT	C. Stadler & H. Sutton	5 & 4
P. Way & I. Woosnam	LOST TO	C. Strange & P. Jacobsen	4 & 2
B. Langer & K. Brown	BEAT	R. Floyd & L. Wadkins	3 & 2

Score: Europe 9 United States 7

SCORES: DAY THREE

Singles			
M. Pinero	BEAT	L. Wadkins	3 & 1
I. Woosnam	LOST TO	C. Stadler	2 & 1
P. Way	BEAT	R. Floyd	2 holes
S. Ballesteros	HALVED	T. Kite	
A. Lyle	BEAT	P. Jacobsen	3 & 2
B. Langer	BEAT	H. Sutton	5 & 4
S. Torrance	BEAT	A. North	1 hole
H. Clark	BEAT	M. O'Meara	1 hole
N. Faldo	LOST TO	H. Green	3 & 1
J. Rivero	LOST TO	C. Peete	1 hole
J-M. Canizares	BEAT	F. Zoeller	2 holes
K. Brown	LOST TO	C. Strange	4 & 2

Final Score: Europe 16½ United States 11½

Tony Jacklin has enjoyed some great moments in golf but he admitted that captaining this team gave him the greatest satisfaction. 'To be part of this sort of thing is something I can hardly speak about,' he said. 'We made history today. For me the dream finishes like that.'

Jacklin's team of experience and youth won the Ryder Cup in true lionhearted fashion even if Ray Floyd was disturbed at Paul Way's refusal to give him that easy putt, and even if Lee Trevino was not happy about the partisanship of the British fans. But excuses cannot be offered or accepted: the better team won.

The Ryder Cup had been a long time returning to Britain, 28 years in fact, and it ended yet another American sporting monopoly, just as Australia had done with the America's Cup two years earlier.

But Lee Trevino was one man who knew how large his task was going to be when, seven months before the event upon his appointment as US Captain, he said: 'The job of non-playing captain will give me more than enough worries. The days of a cinch win for America are over.' How right he was!

Top: The jubilant winners get their hands on the trophy for the first time since 1957.
Above: The two non-playing captains Lee Trevino (left) and Tony Jacklin. It's clear to see which one won!

THE GOLDEN BEAR DEFIES THE YEARS

'Not been playing well enough lately to be considered. But he cannot be brushed aside since the majors have always brought out the best in him.' That was the opinion of Gordon S. White junior, discussing Jack Nicklaus' prospects in his preview of the 1986 Masters in the *New York Times*. Another factor White was not aware of when making his assessment was that 1986 was to be the 'Year of the Geriatric.'

Nicklaus had won the Masters a record five times and since his last win in 1975 he had come close to making it number six on two occasions – in 1977 when Tom Watson beat him by two strokes and in 1981 when he tied second with Johnny Miller, again behind Watson. Although Gordon White was correct in saying you could never write off Nicklaus, what form did he have coming into the 50th Masters? He had dropped to an unprecedented 44th in the money list in 1985 and his best result was equal second in the Canadian Open and second in the Greater Milwaukee Open Tournament. He had not won on the tour since the Memorial Tournament at Muirfield in 1984 and, more important, he had not won a major since 1980 when he won the PGA and US Open.

Nicklaus was up against the new breed of golfer. There was the top European trio of Bernhard Langer and Severiano Ballesteros, both former Masters champions, and Sandy Lyle, who won the previous week's tournament, the Greater Greensboro Open at Forest Oaks, a similar course to Augusta. The new Sony World Rankings were issued just before the Masters and they had Langer, Ballesteros and Lyle as 1-2-3, but home-bred professionals like Curtis Strange, Calvin Peete and Lanny Wadkins were all lurking in the wings ready to bring the title back into American hands. Tom Watson was also showing signs of coming out of his two-year slump and Andy Bean, Mark O'Meara and Payne Stewart were all in form, and each was looking for his first major. Sadly the reigning US Open champion, Andy North, was unable to play because a chipped bone in his right thumb resulted in his last-minute withdrawal.

Most of the pre-tournament attention was centred around Severiano Ballesteros who came to Augusta with a point to prove. He wanted to show US Tour Commissioner Deane Beman he was wrong in refusing him his ticket for 1986. The best way to do that was for Ballesteros to go out and win his third Masters title. But fellow European Bernhard Langer had enjoyed his taste of success in 1985 and he

Above: The man who came close to winning all four majors in 1986, Greg Norman.
Right: South African Nick Price, playing his second to the 18th, shot a Masters record 63 in the third round.

wanted that green jacket again. Ballesteros had only played nine competitive rounds in 1986 and only 36 holes of US golf, in New Orleans. And, if he was going to win his third title, he would have to master the very fast greens.

The setting was immaculate for the 50th playing of this great event and the course looked as beautiful as ever, although its 6905 yards offered its usual treachery. It suited big hitters with the ability to draw the ball; Ballesteros, Langer and Lyle all fitted that bill. Brilliant sunshine was accompanied by a chilly wind on the opening day which made the greens even faster than expected. The uphill putts were tolerable, but the downhillers were murder – ask Fred Couples. He had a 10-footer for an eagle two at the second. He could not believe his eyes as it sailed 40 feet past the cup and nearly off the green. Amazingly he sank the return for a birdie!

Page 84: Australia's 'Great White Shark' Greg Norman, who led going into the final round at Augusta, just as he did in all the other majors in 1986.

Page 85: Japan's Tommy Nakajima was up with the leaders for three rounds.

Ballesteros broke par with a 71 in the opening round but Langer (two over) and Lyle (four over) found the greens too fast. Nicklaus had two 37s for a two-over 74 but the first-day leaders on 68 were Ken Green and Bill Kratzert.

Kratzert, full name William August Kratzert III, dismissed his caddie James Johnson on the final day of practice because he was late arriving and replaced him by his home-town friend Chuck Hofius. Between them they managed to get round the daunting course in 68 strokes. Kratzert had been in the clubhouse for several hours waiting to see if anybody would share his lead. He was then joined by Ken Green, playing in his first Masters, who had his sister Shelley caddy for him. Green, from Connecticut, is affectionately known on the Tour as 'The Other Green' so as to distinguish him from Hubert Green, and only some remarkable long putting saved his day. He had three bogeys, but 40-foot and 70-foot birdie putts and pars from 30 and 50 feet helped him make a recovery.

The greens remained fast as the wind blew across the course on the second day. 'The Other Green' collapsed and disappeared into the Georgia sun, but Bill Kratzert only dropped one place on the leader board after a par 72 and he was the only US golfer in the first three. The new leader was the Spaniard Ballesteros who made his attack with a four-under par 68. Bubbling with confidence Ballesteros kept the ball under the pin for uphill putts at 16 of the 18 holes but completed his round with a 20-foot downhill putt at

Far left: Despite finishing 68-68 Tom Kite could not overhaul the 'Golden Bear.'
Left: Bernhard Langer started the final day as one of the favorites but slipped away.
Above: The eventual winner, Jack Nicklaus.

the 18th. His big rival Langer moved into contention with a classy 68 and Greg Norman joined Langer on 142 despite four putts for a double bogey at the 10th. Tom Watson had looked like becoming the new leader when he was four under at the 10th but he came to grief with a triple bogey six at the 12th after finding water, and then sand. He finished with a 72, five strokes behind Ballesteros.

The field was reduced to 48 at the half-way stage and among the famous names to miss the cut were Gary Player, Arnold Palmer, Hale Irwin, Isao Aoki and Ray Floyd. Floyd was, however, to have his moment of glory later in the summer when he joined the 'Geriatric Brigade' by winning the Open at Shinnecock Hills. His fellow 'Geriatric', Nicklaus, easily made the cut after his second round 71 gave him a two-round total of 145. But at the half-way stage there were few who believed Jack could pull it off.

Ballesteros allowed his position to slip slightly in the third round as his par 72 let in Australian Greg Norman whose 68 gave him a one-stroke lead over the Spaniard with a three-round total of 210. Joining Ballesteros on 211 was South African Nick Price who wrote his name into the Masters' record books with a new championship record 63, thus beating the 64

Below: Nicklaus in conversation with Sandy Lyle as they walk off the 18th . . . now for the agonising wait.

which had stood since being first registered by Lloyd Mangrum in 1940. Langer was also level with Ballesteros and the sole American representative among the leading five players was Donnie Hammond from Daytona Beach, Florida. Tom Kite and Tom Watson, however, were just one behind and ready to help Hammond stamp out the overseas threat.

Jack Nicklaus had a third round 69 for 214, the same as Sandy Lyle. Nicklaus and Lyle were to play the final 18 holes together, the first time in their careers they had played together. It was certainly to be a memorable round for both men.

Greg Norman had a couple of final-round disasters. First at the eighth when he went into the trees, and then at the 10th where he took a six. Those errors allowed Ballesteros to re-take the lead which he gradually increased. He was nine under with four to play and when he stepped on to the 15th tee he was three up on Nicklaus, who was making one of his famous

charges. When the Spaniard stepped off the 15th he and Nicklaus were level!

A few minutes earlier Nicklaus had hit a four-iron second shot at the 15th to within 12 feet of the pin and he had the same putt as the day in 1975 when he was engaged in that epic battle with Tom Weiskopf and Johnny Miller. He remembered the putt stopped short that day. This time there was no such mistake and he sank the putt for an eagle three. At the next hole, a 170-yard par three, his tee shot was stone dead just four feet away and it was to be a birdie. The noise from the crowd was deafening and that alone was enough to put Ballesteros off. Nicklaus birdied the 17th and then parred 18 to come in nine under on 279. He was then left with a nerve-racking wait in the Bobby Jones Cabin while he watched proceedings on television along with his son Jack, junior, who had been his caddy all week.

While Nicklaus had been hauling himself into the tournament at 15, 16 and 17, Ballesteros was going through one of those nightmares. His four-iron second at the 15th landed in the water and then he bogeyed 16 and, in two holes, he had turned a four-stroke lead over Nicklaus into a one-stroke deficit. In the meantime Australian Norman came back into contention and Tom Kite, who had been playing steady golf, also came into the reckoning.

With Nicklaus safely installed nine-under on 279, it was left to those three to force a play-off or, at the outside, overhaul the great man.

Ballesteros stayed on seven under after pars at the 17th and 18th but Kite and Norman were still capable of catching Nicklaus as they came to the 18th. Kite was first to play the final hole in this great drama. He had an 11-foot putt to tie Nicklaus and it was obvious he was trying hard to win his first major, but the putt missed. There only remained the Australian and what a time he chose for yet another piece of his erratic play! His second shot was awful, just as his second had been at the last hole in the 1984 US Open at Winged Foot which cost him the title. This latest piece of mistiming was to cost him another major. His second was pushed into the grandstand and he had to get down in two to tie. He missed a 10-foot putt for the tie and so Nicklaus was champion for a record sixth time.

In all his years on the golf scene, even Jack could not have believed he would have been involved in such a finish. Not only did he win his 20th major title but, at the age of 46, he became the oldest winner of the Masters. Maybe Gordon S. White, junior, will have a re-think when reviewing the 51st Masters – you can never say Jack Nicklaus is not playing well enough to be considered. He always has that piece of magic up his sleeve!

Left: Despite the years, Nicklaus still has that desire to win.
Right: Nick Price on the 18th, establishing the new Masters record.

CARD OF COURSE

Hole	Name	Yards	Par
1	Tea Olive	400	4
2	Pink Dogwood	555	5
3	Flowering Peach	360	4
4	Crabapple	205	3
5	Magnolia	435	4
6	Juniper	180	3
7	Pampas	360	4
8	Yellow Jasmine	535	5
9	Carolina Cherry	435	4
Out		**3465**	**36**
10	Camellia	485	4
11	White Dogwood	455	4
12	Golden Bell	155	3
13	Azalea	465	5
14	Chinese Fir	405	4
15	Firethorn	500	5
16	Red Bud	170	3
17	Nandina	400	4
18	Holly	405	4
In		**3440**	**36**
Total		**6905**	**72**

NICKLAUS' 20 MAJORS
1959 US Amateur
1961 US Amateur
1962 US Open
1963 PGA, Masters
1965 Masters
1966 British Open, Masters
1967 US Open
1970 British Open
1971 PGA
1972 US Open, Masters
1973 PGA
1975 Masters, PGA
1978 British Open
1980 US Open, PGA
1986 Masters

ROUND THREE LEADERS
210 Greg Norman 70-72-68
211 Nick Price 79-69-63
211 Donnie Hammond 73-71-67
211 Bernhard Langer 74-68-69
211 Severiano Ballesteros 71-68-72
212 Tom Kite 70-74-68
212 Tom Watson 70-74-68
212 Tommy Nakajima 70-71-71
214 **Jack Nicklaus** 74-71-69

FINAL SCORES
279 **Jack Nicklaus** 74-71-69-65
280 Greg Norman 70-72-68-70
280 Tom Kite 70-74-68-68
281 Severiano Ballesteros 71-68-72-70
282 Nick Price 79-69-63-71
283 Tom Watson 70-74-68-71
283 Jay Haas 76-69-71-67

Top left: Surely even Jack did not think he would be wearing the famous green jacket for the sixth time, particularly at the start of the final day?
Left: Tom Kite's agony at missing at the 18th and failing to tie with Nicklaus.
Right: This birdie at the 17th took Nicklaus to a championship-winning nine under par.

THE 1987 RYDER CUP

Tony Jacklin was first entrusted with the job of captaining the European Ryder Cup Team in 1983. At the PGA National, Palm Beach Gardens, he came close to leading his European side to an historic victory because the United States had never lost on home soil. On that occasion a home victory was secured thanks to the experience of Tom Watson winning the final singles against Bernard Gallacher. Jacklin had to return home with his band of heroes after coming within one point of wresting the coveted trophy from the American team.

Lee Trevino, the American captain in 1985, knew that attempting to keep hold of the trophy they had not lost in 28 years would not be easy on British soil. The days of the guaranteed American win had long gone. And in the two years since the close call at the PGA National, Sandy Lyle had become the first home winner of the British Open since Jacklin in 1969, and Bernhard Langer had won the Masters against the best of the Americans at Augusta.

Any anxiety the American team may have felt proved well-founded when, at the Belfry, the home of the British PGA, Tony Jacklin and his men showed what a force European golf had become in the 1980s – the European team inflicted a five-point defeat upon their rivals from across the Atlantic for the first time since 1957 when Dai Rees captained the British team to a fine victory at Lindrick.

Jacklin, frequently an idol for British fans, had become a hero again. He had enjoyed great personal triumph in 1969 when he won the British Open at Royal Lytham, and less than a year later he completed a notable double when he destroyed the American challenge, to win the US Open at Hazeltine, Minnesota, by seven shots from Dave Hill. Those individual triumphs were great moments for Jacklin and ones the British public shared. His influence on the game was great and it inspired many young people to take up the game. But in winning the Ryder Cup, Jacklin enjoyed a moment as

Below: A huge gallery of rival fans was there to support the European and American teams in the 1987 Ryder Cup.

great as his individual triumphs. He knew he had won the trophy for his country, and that knowledge gave him great pleasure.

But Tony Jacklin had further ambitions. He wanted to take his team to the United States and win the Ryder Cup on American soil. That feat had never been performed in 26 matches over 60 years of the Ryder Cup. It was a tall order, but Jacklin relished the challenge.

America's captain when the team had last played on home soil, in 1983, was the nation's favorite golfing son, Jack Nicklaus. Jack had himself enjoyed another great moment in his long and successful career in 1986 when he became the oldest winner of the Masters. He won the title for the sixth time, thus returning the title to the United States after the period of Bernhard Langer's temporary ownership.

The American team saw Jack as the man to repair the damaged pride of defeat at the Belfry, and when it was announced that the 1987 match would be played over the 7104-yard Muirfield Village course near Columbus, Ohio, the American team was given an even greater advantage – the course had been designed by none other than the 'Golden Bear.'

The European team was more experienced in terms of Ryder Cup appearances and only Jose-Maria Olazabal and Gordon Brand Junior had not played in the Ryder Cup before. Nine of the other ten players were members of that victorious side at the Belfry two years earlier, Eamonn Darcy being the odd man out. Three British Open winners, including the 1987 champion Nick Faldo, were in the European team and Ken Brown was added as one of Tony Jacklin's three personal choices because of the vast and useful experience he had gained while playing on the US Tour.

Men like Tom Watson had long since gone from the US team which now faced the match with no fewer than five debutants – Mark Calcavecchia, Larry Mize, Dan Pohl, Scott Simpson, and the colorful Payne Stewart. But in Ben Crenshaw, Andy Bean, Tom Kite, Curtis Strange, Hal Sutton and Lanny Wadkins the American team had six of the biggest names in golf and six of the biggest money-winners of all time. All had career winnings of over $2 million. Despite Europe's obvious advantage of Ryder Cup experience, the United States still started as favorites to win on their own soil.

The first morning foursomes opened with an all-too-familiar sight. The Americans were leading in all four matches and it looked as though the euphoria of a European win was going to fall flat. Top money-winner Curtis Strange and Tom Kite opened the scoring for the United States by beating Sam Torrance, the hero at the Belfry in 1985, and Howard Clark; then Brown and Langer lost to Hal Sutton and Dan Pohl.

Europe were two down and it was looking grim but the turning point came when Faldo and top European money-winner Ian Woosnam came from four down to beat Lanny Wadkins and Larry Mize by two holes; then Ballesteros and newcomer Jose-Maria Olazabal recovered from two down after five to beat Larry Nelson and Payne Stewart. At lunch on the first day the teams were

Above: The Spanish pairing of Seve Ballesteros and Jose-Maria Olazabal (right) proved outstanding in the fourballs and foursomes. They won three of their four matches.

level at 2-2, but the Europeans must have been riding high on a wave of confidence after their recovery, and it certainly showed in the afternoon as they won every one of the fourball matches.

Gordon Brand and Jose Rivero settled in like old hands, and beat Crenshaw and Scott Simpson 3 & 2. Then Langer and Lyle staged a great recovery, after being two down with five to play, to win by one hole against Andy Bean who was playing his first match for eight years, and Mark Calcavecchia. Woosnam and Faldo beat Sutton and Dan Pohl to make it 5-2, and Ballesteros and his young Spanish partner Olazabal completed the agony for the home team by beating Strange and Kite. Ballesteros had been the influencing factor in the European camp, and on these occasions he tends to play like a man possessed. He wanted to win the cup as much as any man in the European team.

Strange and Kite brought the American team back into the reckoning during the second day's foursomes by beating Rivero and Brand, and then Sutton and Mize stopped the European team from increasing their lead further by halving with Faldo and Woosnam. But Lyle and Langer proved too good for Wadkins and Nelson, while Ballesteros and Olazabal sneaked a one-hole win against Crenshaw and Payne Stewart, thanks to Seve holing a pressure-putt from seven feet at the 18th.

Halfway through the match Europe led 8½-3½, but this is golf. It is an unpredictable game and nobody knew that better than Jacklin. That five-point lead was maintained in the afternoon fourballs that prompted Jacklin to comment: 'I never thought I would see the day when I would see golf played like this.'

Bean and Stewart went out in a better ball 29 as they beat Darcy and Brand 3 & 2. Ahead of them Faldo and Woosnam destroyed the top American pairing of Strange and Kite, and when the match ended at the 14th the European pair were 10-under par. Both pairs opened with five consecutive birdies which Nicklaus described as 'just not on' for a course that is supposed to be one of the toughest in America. At the 441-yard 10th Woosnam hit a drive, then a wedge to within three feet of the flag. How could players even of Strange and Kite's caliber match that?

Olazabal and Ballesteros lost their first match in four outings but not until Seve had shown all his wizardry in doing everything except stop Sutton and Mize from winning. But the most memorable of the afternoon fourballs was the match between Lyle and Langer, and Wadkins and Nelson.

A magnificent 246-yard shot with a two-iron by Lyle at the par-5 11th set up an eagle and a one-hole lead. The European pair never lost that lead. They went three up with three to play after Lyle conjured up another eagle at the 15th. But Wadkins came back with birdies at the 16th and 17th to reduce the lead to one. The pressure was on Langer and Lyle

Wadkins produced another magnificent shot, nearly hitting his second at the 18th into the hole, but Langer matched Wadkins' shot and this was good enough to secure another European win. That win was to turn out vitally important as the match went into the final day.

The singles were dramatic, the tension almost unbearable at times. Twenty-five thousand fervent American fans packed the Ohio course. Europe only needed 3½ points out of 12 singles to retain the cup and 4 points to become the first team to win on American soil.

The first five matches all went to the 18th hole. At the top of the order Andy Bean played Ian Woosnam and stood a good 12 inches taller than the Welshman. But off the tee there was little to choose as Woosnam matched his American opponent for length. Bean was two up at the turn and Woosnam missed a chance to level it at the 14th. At the 17th the European let another chance slip as Bean put himself into trouble off the tee. Woosnam struggled to hold on for a five and stay only one down but he cold not muster a match-halving birdie at the last and the Americans started the singles with a win.

In contrast Howard Clark·took advantage of a bit of good fortune at the 18th against Dan Pohl. After a bad hook he was allowed a drop because of interference from a television cable and he had a direct shot at the green. He found the green and Pohl played through the green and into a bunker. Clark won the hole and in so doing he succeeded in restoring the lead to five points.

Above: Despite losing only one of his five matches, Hal Sutton could do very little to stop a European triumph.

Larry Mize halved with Sam Torrance, the man who had won the match for Europe at the Belfry two years earlier, and then there was a run of US wins that set the alarm bells ringing in the European camp.

Nick Faldo was the hot favorite to beat the newcomer Mark Calcavecchia and was one up at the turn. Playing his worst golf since winning the Open, Faldo then lost the long 11th and 14th and ran out the loser by one hole. American fans went wild with excitement and in quick succession the cheers rang out from all corners of the course as their heroes started picking up holes.

The young Spaniard Olazabal had enjoyed his first Ryder Cup match and in his singles against Payne Stewart was all square at the halfway stage. The American went ahead with a par at the 16th and held on to win by one at the 18th hole, but Olazabal was far from disgraced on his debut.

Sandy Lyle went down 3 & 2 to Tom Kite. Another Spaniard Jose Rivero, looked 'dead' at the turn when trailing Scott Simpson by two, but pulled back to level it. But with birdies at the 15th and 16th, the American team went on to clinch victory. Suddenly the score read: United States 11, Europe 12. Then luck changed for the European team when Irishman Eamonn Darcy won his first ever Ryder Cup match.

Three up against Ben Crenshaw, Darcy must have wondered what was happening when Crenshaw went one up, particularly as Crenshaw was putting with a one-iron or wedge after breaking his putter in a fit of anger when he missed a putt at the sixth hole. Despite being without a putter Crenshaw managed three successive birdies from the 12th. But Darcy showed the spirit that was flowing through the European camp. He won

SCORES: DAY ONE

United States		Europe	
Foursomes			
C. Strange & T. Kite	BEAT	S. Torrance & H. Clark	4 & 2
H. Sutton & D. Pohl	BEAT	K. Brown & B. Langer	2 & 1
L. Wadkins & L. Mize	LOST TO	N. Faldo & I. Woosnam	2 holes
L. Nelson & P. Stewart	LOST TO	S. Ballesteros & J-M. Olazabal	1 hole
Fourballs			
B. Crenshaw & S. Simpson	LOST TO	G. Brand, Jr & J. Rivero	3 & 2
A. Bean & M. Calcavecchia	LOST TO	S. Lyle & B. Langer	1 hole
H. Sutton & D. Pohl	LOST TO	I. Woosnam & N. Faldo	2 & 1
C. Strange & T. Kite	LOST TO	S. Ballesteros & J-M. Olazabal	2 & 1

Score: Europe 6 United States 2

SCORES: DAY TWO

Foursomes			
C. Strange & T. Kite	BEAT	J. Rivero & G. Brand Jr	2 & 1
H. Sutton & L. Mize	HALVED WITH	N. Faldo & I. Woosnam	
L. Wadkins & L. Nelson	LOST TO	S. Lyle & B. Langer	2 & 1
B. Crenshaw & P. Stewart	LOST TO	S. Ballesteros & J-M. Olazabal	1 hole
Fourballs			
C. Strange & T. Kite	LOST TO	N. Faldo & I. Woosnam	5 & 4
A. Bean & P. Stewart	BEAT	E. Darcy & G. Brand Jr	3 & 2
H. Sutton & L. Mize	BEAT	S. Ballesteros & J-M. Olazabal	2 & 1
L. Wadkins & L. Nelson	LOST TO	S. Lyle & B. Langer	1 hole

Score: Europe 10½ United States 5½

SCORES: DAY THREE

Singles			
A. Bean	BEAT	I. Woosnam	1 hole
D. Pohl	LOST TO	H. Clark	1 hole
L. Mize	HALVED WITH	S. Torrance	
M. Calcavecchia	BEAT	N. Faldo	1 hole
P. Stewart	BEAT	J-M. Olazabal	1 hole
S. Simpson	BEAT	J. Rivero	2 & 1
T. Kite	BEAT	S. Lyle	3 & 2
B. Crenshaw	LOST TO	E. Darcy	1 hole
L. Nelson	HALVED WITH	B. Langer	
C. Strange	LOST TO	S. Ballesteros	2 & 1
L. Wadkins	BEAT	K. Brown	3 & 2
H. Sutton	HALVED WITH	G. Brand Jr	

Final Score: Europe 15 United States 13

the 17th to level the match and then blasted out of a bunker to give himself a three-foot putt for the match at the last hole. A miss could have seen the putt go five feet past the hole but to the delight of Darcy, Tony Jacklin and millions of British fans watching on television, the putt went in. Darcy had restored Europe's lead to two, with four matches still out on the course. It seemed unlikely that Langer and Ballesteros would lose their matches – but no one could be sure.

Nelson led the German by three after 11 holes, but after three successive birdies from the 12th the pair finished their match in halves, and when they conceded each other's putt at the 18th, it effectively meant that Europe had retained the Ryder Cup because Ballesteros was in a dormie position against Curtis Strange. But Jacklin and Ballesteros wanted to *win*, not *draw* the match. Seve had been three up early in the match but by the 13th Strange had cut that deficit to one. Ballesteros edged ahead by one more at the 14th and at the 17th he sealed a great win for himself and his team. The Ryder Cup had been lost on American soil for the first time.

The two matches still out on the course were academic. Lanny Wadkins beat Ken Brown 3 & 2 and Gordon Brand and Hal Sutton halved the last match. The celebrations had already begun.

Jose-Maria Olazabal was seen dancing his way across the 18th green. Tony Jacklin flitted from each of his heroes in turn to offer his congratulations. He was dazed, numbed. It took a long while for the significance of the European win to sink in. When Jacklin had a microphone thrust in front of him, the normally elo-

Top: The victorious European team of (left to right, back row) Seve Ballesteros, Gordon Brand, Sandy Lyle, Tony Jacklin, Nick Faldo, Sam Torrance, Eamonn Darcy; (front row) Jose Rivero, Jose-Maria Olazabal, Ken Brown, Ian Woosnam, Bernhard Langer and Howard Clark.
Above: Jack Nicklaus celebrates with Tony Jacklin (right), captain of the winning 1987 European Ryder Cup team.

quent golfer was speechless – his tears did all the talking for him. Jack Nicklaus, generous in defeat as always, was the first to acknowledge that the better team had won and deserved the victory.

Tony Jacklin has enjoyed some great moments in golf. No man has ever led his country with greater pride. His team deserved the victory. Tony Jacklin deserved his success at Muirfield Village in 1987.

Picture Credits

All-Sport: pages 2-3, 6, 31 (top), 46, 47, 48 (bottom), 51 (top), 57 (bottom), 63 (both), 67, 68 (top), 69 (both), 74-75, 76, 76, 77, 78, 81, 83, 84, 85, 86 (right), 87, 90, 91, 92 (both), 93, 94, 95, 98(both).

Associated Press: 21 (top), 23, 25 (bottom), 32, 37, 44 (bottom), 45 (both), 60 (both).

BBC Hulton Picture Library/Bettman Archive: pages 18, 22 (right), 25 (top right).

BBC Hulton Picture Library: pages 4-5, 8, 10, 12 (bottom), 13 (bottom), 14, 16, 33, 34, 40 (both), 41 (both).

Frank Christian Studios: pages 9, 30 (top), 54 (top).

Brian Morgan, Golf Photography International: pages 7 (right), 31,

(bottom), 61, 70, 72-73, 79, 81 (bottom), 82, 86 (left), 88, 96.

The Bert Neale Collection: pages 1, 7 (left), 19, 20, 21 (bottom), 24, 25 (top left), 26, 27 (top), 30 (bottom), 36 (both), 38 (both), 39 (both), 42, 43, 44 (top), 48 (top), 49, 50, 51 (bottom), 55, 56, 57 (top), 58, 59, 62, 64, 66, 68 (bottom).

TPS/Central Press: pages 12 (top), 17, 22 (left).

TPS/CLI: page 35 (both).

TPS/Fox: page 13 (top).

TPS/Keystone: pages 28-29, 54 (bottom)

Bob Thomas Sports Photography: pages 65.

US Golf Association: page 27 (bottom).